Teach Yourself
VISUALLY™

iPad® 2

Visual

Lonzell Watson

WILEY

Teach Yourself VISUALLY™ iPad® 2

Published by
Wiley Publishing, Inc.
10475 Crosspoint Boulevard
Indianapolis, IN 46256

www.wiley.com

Published simultaneously in Canada

Wiley also publishes its books in a variety of electronic formats and by print-on-demand. Some content that appears in standard print versions of this book may not be available in other formats. For more information about Wiley products, visit us at www.wiley.com.

Library of Congress Control Number: 2011930302

ISBN: 978-1-118-05415-4

Manufactured in the United States of America

10 9 8 7 6 5 4 3 2 1

Trademark Acknowledgments

Contact Us

For general information on our other products and services please contact our Customer Care Department within the U.S. at 877-762-2974, outside the U.S. at 317-572-3993, or fax 317-572-4002.

For technical support please visit www.wiley.com/techsupport.

WILEY Sales | Contact Wiley at (877) 762-2974 or fax (317) 572-4002.

Credits

Acquisitions Editor
Aaron Black

Sr. Project Editor
Sarah Hellert

Technical Editor
Dennis R. Cohen

Copy Editor
Scott Tullis

Editorial Director
Robyn Siesky

Business Manager
Amy Knies

Sr. Marketing Manager
Sandy Smith

Vice President and Executive Group Publisher
Richard Swadley

Vice President and Executive Publisher
Barry Pruett

Project Coordinator
Sheree Montgomery

Graphics and Production Specialists
Andrea Hornberger
Heather Pope

Quality Control Technician
Lindsay Amones

Proofreader
Mildred Rosenzweig

Indexer
BIM Indexing & Proofreading Services

Screen Artist
Ana Carrillo

Illustrator
Ronda David-Burroughs

About the Author

Lonzell Watson is the award-winning author of *Teach Yourself VISUALLY iPad*, for which he won the 2011 International Award of Excellence. His work also earned him the Distinguished Technical Communication award and Best of Show 2010 from the Society for Technical Communication. Lonzell was also presented the Award of Excellence for *Teach Yourself VISUALLY iPhoto '09* in 2009. He is the author of other popular titles, including *Canon VIXIA HD Camcorder Digital Field Guide*, *Final Cut Pro 6 for Digital Video Editors Only*, and *Teach Yourself VISUALLY Digital Video*.

Lonzell is an Adjunct Professor in the College of Business at Bellevue University and a freelance technical writer and instructional designer whose courseware has been used to train the CIA, FBI, NASA, and all branches of the U.S. Armed Forces. He is a frequent contributor to StudioMonthly.com. Hundreds of Lonzell's tutorials and tips that help demystify consumer electronics and software have been syndicated. He holds a master's degree in Instructional Design and Development and is the owner of Creative Intelligence LLC, an instructional design and technical writing company (creativeintel.com).

Author's Acknowledgments

I would like to give special thanks to Aaron Black, without whom this project would not have been possible. I would also like to thank project editor Sarah Hellert whose organizational precision and demand for excellence has made this book a truly creative and wonderful way to learn how to get the most from iPad 2. I would also like to thank the graphics department for their outstanding work articulating complex concepts through amazing visual works of art. I would also like to thank technical editor Dennis Cohen for overseeing the accuracy for exercises in this book.

Special thanks go to Laura Clor, to my lovely wife, Robyn, to Shannon Johnson, Danya and Sean Platt, and Kimmi and James Patterson for their assistance as I wrote this book.

I dedicate this book to Evelyn Wenzel, to whom I am forever grateful.

How to Use This Book

Who This Book Is For

This book is for the reader who has never used this particular technology or software application. It is also for readers who want to expand their knowledge.

The Conventions in This Book

① Steps

This book uses a step-by-step format to guide you easily through each task. **Numbered steps** are actions you must do; **bulleted steps** clarify a point, step, or optional feature; and **indented steps** give you the result.

② Notes

Notes give additional information — special conditions that may occur during an operation, a situation that you want to avoid, or a cross-reference to a related area of the book.

③ Icons and Buttons

Icons and buttons show you exactly what you need to click to perform a step.

④ Tips

Tips offer additional information, including warnings and shortcuts.

⑤ Bold

Bold type shows command names or options that you must click or text or numbers you must type.

⑥ Italics

Italic type introduces and defines a new term.

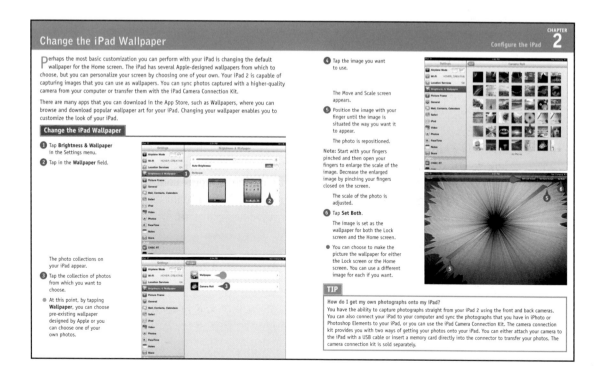

Table of Contents

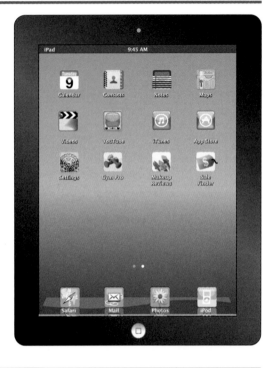

Chapter 3 Get the Most Out of the Internet

Chapter 4 Maximize Email on the iPad

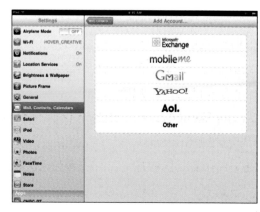

Table of Contents

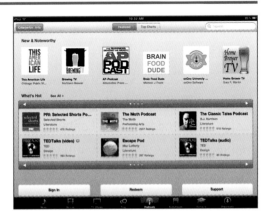

Chapter 7   Get the Most from YouTube and iBooks

Chapter 8   Manage Contacts and Appointments

Table of Contents

Chapter 9 Simplify Your Life with the iPad

Chapter 10 — Enhance Your iPad

Chapter 11 — Maintain and Troubleshoot the iPad

CHAPTER 1

Get to Know the iPad

This chapter acquaints you with one of the most highly anticipated electronic devices of all time: the iPad. The iPad is an amazingly powerful work of technological art, renowned for its large, high-resolution, multi-touch screen and overall sleek design. This chapter gives you an extensive tour of the many features that have made the iPad the talk of the town.

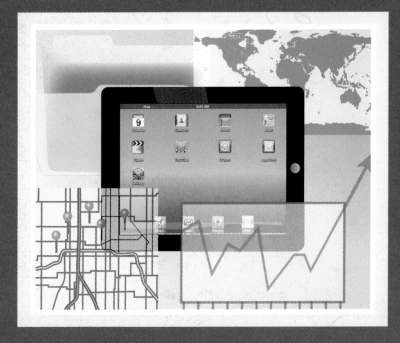

Take a Look at the iPad

The iPad is elegantly designed, easy to use, and amazingly powerful. The iPad is capable of performing many of the tasks that you may require from your MacBook, MacBook Pro, or PC, including surfing the web, exchanging emails, desktop publishing, downloading apps, and playing video games.

Before you learn the many features and tasks you can perform with your iPad, take the time to become familiar with the iPad's layout. If you already use an iPhone or iPod touch, then you should feel quite at home with the iPad. Becoming familiar with the iPad hardware is important so you can take advantage of everything the iPad offers.

iPad Overview

The iPad is a portable hardware device hybridizing the iPhone and a laptop. The large LED backlit display acts as both monitor and keyboard. The iPad operating system and multi-touch screen is the same that is used on the iPhone, where you use gestures to scroll, rotate, and zoom in on objects. Almost every iPhone app in the App Store works on the iPad.

iPad 2 Technical Specifications

The iPad has a 9.7-inch screen and a 1024×768 pixel resolution at 132 pixels per inch. The iPad 2 uses a 1GHz Apple A5 dual-core custom processor and comes in three storage capacities: 16GB, 32GB, and 64GB flash drives. The iPad can access Wi-Fi networks as well as cellular networks with its 3G model.

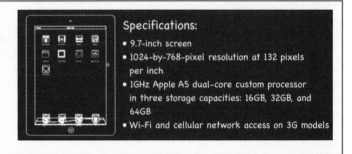

Specifications:
- 9.7-inch screen
- 1024-by-768-pixel resolution at 132 pixels per inch
- 1GHz Apple A5 dual-core custom processor in three storage capacities: 16GB, 32GB, and 64GB
- Wi-Fi and cellular network access on 3G models

iPad Design and Buttons

● Front Camera

You can use the front camera for the new FaceTime video calling feature. FaceTime for iPad enables you to make video calls from your iPad 2 to a friend's iPad, iPhone, iPod touch, or Intel-based Mac. The front camera lets you see your friend and lets your friend see you.

● Multi-Touch Screen

You use the touch screen to access everything on the iPad with just a tap of your finger. Gestures are used to scroll, rotate, and zoom in on objects on-screen. The display is also used to view content in portrait or landscape orientation when you physically turn it.

Home Button

The Home button acts as a starting point for many of the functions you perform with the iPad, including bringing the iPad out of Sleep mode, accessing Spotlight, and returning you to the Home screen.

Headphone Jack

You can insert your own personal headphones into the headphone jack to listen to music, watch videos, and play games in privacy. The headphone jack also supports iPhone-compatible headphone-microphone combos.

On/Off, Sleep/Wake

You can use this button in conjunction with the Home button to turn off the iPad. You can press this button to place the iPad into Sleep mode and to bring the iPad out of Sleep mode.

Back Camera

You can use the back camera for the new FaceTime video calling feature to capture photographs and record HD (720p) video. The FaceTime app on your iPad 2 enables you to switch from the front camera to the back camera so that you can show your surroundings during your video conference.

Silent/Screen Rotation Lock

You can use the Silent button as a quick and easy way to mute all sounds on the iPad or to lock the iPad's screen into its current orientation: portrait or landscape.

Volume Up/Down

You can use the Volume Up/Down buttons to raise and lower the volume of the iPad.

Built-In Speaker

The built-in speaker enables the iPad to play back audio without accessories, such as headphones or external speakers.

30-Pin Connector

The 30-pin connector enables you to attach the iPad to the iPad dock in order to charge it. You can use this connector to connect to a computer as well as to other iPad accessories, such as the camera connection kit.

Discover iPad 2 Features

The iPad is a combination entertainment center, highly productive office tool, and educational device. Not only can you enjoy great-sounding audio and high-resolution video playback, but you can also capture HD video and high-quality photos. You can teach a classroom from an app or conduct a presentation using Keynote via video mirroring to a big screen.

iPad 2 is chock full of new features that improve upon the performance and productivity of its predecessor. Understanding the key features of the iPad is important so you can best plan how it can serve you.

Capture Images and Video Conference

iPad 2 is equipped with two video cameras, which means you can now enjoy some of the features you have enjoyed on your Mac and iPhone 4, such as video conferencing. What this also means is that you can capture photos and HD (720p) videos straight from your iPad. iPad 2 is now equipped with the Photo Booth app so that you can take snapshots of you and your friends with some artsy effects.

Rotate to Portrait or Landscape

The ability to rotate your screen between portrait and landscape orientation and have iPad adjust the screen is nothing new for iPad. What is new for iPad 2 is that the new accelerometer, three-axis gyroscope, and compass all work together. iPad 2 has a better sense of direction and how it is moving than the original iPad. What this means for you is that games, maps, and other apps can know every tilt and rotation you make with the iPad 2, for higher-performing apps.

Multitask and Create Folders

iOS 4.3 enables you to be more productive by allowing you to run multiple apps simultaneously and easily switch between them. iOS 4.3 also helps you to organize your apps by enabling you to create and name folders in which you can store them. This is a great way to help you keep your Home screens clutter free.

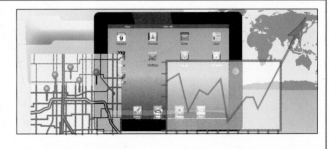

Use Video Mirroring

You can use the optional Apple Digital AV Adapter or Apple VGA Adapter to connect your iPad 2 to your HDTV or projector. The new video-mirroring features enable you to showcase any app, web page, video, movie, or presentation to a large audience by turning your HDTV or projector into a larger version of your iPad.

Print Wirelessly

You can print straight from your iPad 2 using Wi-Fi to any AirPrint-supported printer. You do not need to download any drivers or connect any cables. When you are ready to print, your iPad automatically detects any AirPrint-enabled devices so that you can print movie tickets, web pages, PDFs, presentations, and more.

Get Some AirPlay

If you have an AppleTV, AirPlay-enabled speakers, or an AirPort Express device, you can play movies, music, and photos wirelessly from your iPad to an HDTV or speakers. Just tap the AirPlay icon while you view your favorite HD videos or photos on your iPad to view them on your HDTV via AppleTV. Your iPad and AppleTV need to be connected to the same Wi-Fi network.

continued ▶

Learn about Battery Life

Even with all of its new features, the iPad has maintained its up-to-ten hours of battery life. Battery life can vary wildly depending on the tasks you perform. Watching videos and playing games uses more power than playing music. Higher brightness levels for the display screen can also use more battery life.

Connect to Wi-Fi and 3G Networks

The iPad has the ability to take advantage of the fastest Wi-Fi networks. The iPad can automatically detect available Wi-Fi networks that you can join. The iPad is also available in a 3G model, so if you happen to be somewhere without a Wi-Fi network, you can still access the web. You can now choose from AT&T or Verizon.

Use Accessories for the iPad

Many accessories have been made for the iPad 2, like protective cases such as the new Smart Cover (works only with iPad 2); the keyboard dock, which features a full-sized keyboard; a stand-alone dock; and a camera connection kit for importing photos from a camera or SD card. The iPad also comes with Bluetooth 2.1 + EDR technology, allowing you to use devices such as wireless headphones and the wireless keyboards.

Play Videos

You can watch HD movies, TV shows, podcasts, music videos, and videos you have captured with your iPad 2 on the high-resolution iPad screen. You can switch between widescreen and full-screen viewing just by double-tapping the viewing area. You can control downloaded videos by using simple player controls, including Rewind, Play, Pause, and Fast Forward, or by simply jumping to the next or previous scenes.

Shop the App Store

The App Store provides you with tens of thousands of apps that you can choose from to enhance the capabilities of your iPad. By tapping the App Store icon on the Home screen, you can choose from over 65,000 apps made for iPad (at the time of this writing), ranging from games to business apps, that enable you to take full advantage of your iPad. Of course, you can still use most apps made specifically for the iPhone and iPod touch on your iPad. The number of iPad-specific apps is growing by the day.

Buy, Download, and Read eBooks

The iPad is also an eReader, with access to thousands of books, ranging from classics to bestsellers, through the iBooks app, Kindle app, Stanza, and other eReaders you can download. Once you download a book, the iBooks app places it on your virtual bookshelf. You can choose books from your bookshelf and read them in sharp clarity, even in low light. You will need to download the free iBooks app from the App Store.

Find Your Way by Using Maps

The iPad also comes with a very helpful Maps app that provides high-resolution maps that can help you find directions. You can pinpoint your current location, bookmark locations, get up close with street view, and even search for nearby landmarks. The Maps app is powered by Google.

Take Notes, Schedule Appointments, and Work with Contacts

The iPad also comes with apps that can help you schedule appointments and manage contacts. You also have the ability to sync the data within these apps to your Mac or Windows PC. The Notes, Calendar, and Contacts apps are great ways for you to stay organized when you are on the go.

Start Up and Log In

Your iPad wakes the moment you press the Home button. Starting your iPad 2 can now be simpler than ever. If you use one of the new Smart Covers, iPad wakes up automatically the moment you pull back the cover.

If you do not use a Smart Cover, you will need to unlock your iPad by sliding the unlock button from left to right to access the iPad features. The iPad is instantly put to sleep when you use the Smart Cover to conceal its display or when you press the Sleep/Wake button. Powering on and off the iPad is an incredibly easy process that you can achieve in just a few simple steps.

Learn about the Home Button

The Home button acts as a starting point for many of the functions you perform with the iPad, and you can also customize its functionality. Its most basic functions are to wake the iPad from sleep and to turn off the iPad while pressing the Sleep/ Wake button in conjunction. You can press the Home button to bring the iPad out of Standby mode so you can unlock the iPad. You also use the Home button to return to the Home screen.

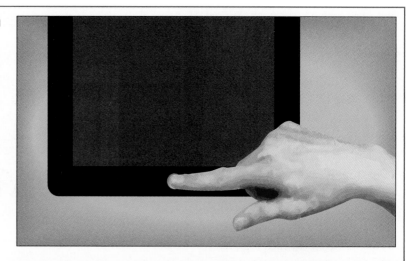

Unlock the iPad

When the iPad is asleep, it is considered locked, rendering any taps on the touch screen and the volume controls unresponsive. This is to protect the iPad from any unwanted taps. After you turn on the iPad or bring it out of Sleep mode by pressing the Home button, you reach the Slide to Unlock screen. Like the iPhone or iPod touch, you can place a finger on the arrow button and slide it to the right to unlock the iPad.

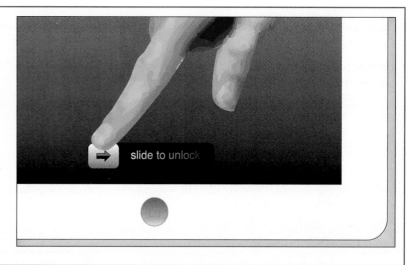

slide to unlock

Protect Your iPad with a Passcode

Unfortunately, simply locking your iPad is not sufficient for protecting your personal effects. Others can also unlock your iPad. You can protect your iPad by designating a passcode that one must type before he or she can gain access to your iPad. Protecting your iPad with a

passcode is a good idea if you have sensitive or confidential information on your iPad. See Chapter 2 for more on setting a passcode for your iPad.

Improve Passcode Complexity

If you prefer a more complex passcode, iOS4 enables you to switch from a simple 4-digit number passcode to a longer alphanumeric passcode. This feature enables you to make it more difficult for someone with ill intentions to randomly guess your simple passcode. To protect the confidential information on your iPad, you can also configure your

iPad to delete all data after a specified number of unsuccessful passcode login attempts.

Shut Down and Sleep

You can power down your iPad by pressing the On/Off button located on the upper right corner of the iPad. You can put your iPad in Sleep mode by pressing the Sleep/Wake button, which also happens to be the On/Off button. Putting the iPad to sleep locks the iPad. A sleeping iPad is still powered. Continue to press the Sleep/Wake button for several seconds to reveal the slide to power off option to power down your iPad.

Explore the iPad Home Screen

The iPad Home screen is the gateway to nearly all the activities you can engage in on the iPad. If you use an iPhone or iPod touch, then you are already well acquainted with how to interface with the iPad. If you are not an iPhone or iPod touch user, you will be comfortable navigating your iPad's interface in just minutes.

Your Home screens were created to be clean, simple, and intuitive for you to use your finger to access all of the amazing features that the iPad has to offer. Knowing the components of the Home screen is important so you can navigate your iPad.

● Home Screen

The Home screen is the starting point for almost everything you can do on the iPad. On the Home screen, you can see and access the icons for all the apps installed on the iPad. You can customize the appearance of the Home screen by changing the wallpaper to another Apple design, or specify a graphic of your own as wallpaper. You can also rearrange the app icons and distribute them across multiple Home screen pages. You can always reset the Home screen layout. See Chapter 2 for more on resetting the Home screen layout for your iPad.

● Dock

The Dock gives you quick access to the apps you use the most, such as Safari, Mail, Photos, and iPod. You can rearrange the order of the icons located on the Dock, but you cannot delete the preinstalled apps located on it. You can also remove the preinstalled apps from the Dock onto the Home screen and put different apps on the Dock. Although the Dock comes with four icons, you can have up to six. Tap any of the icons on the Dock to open the specified app.

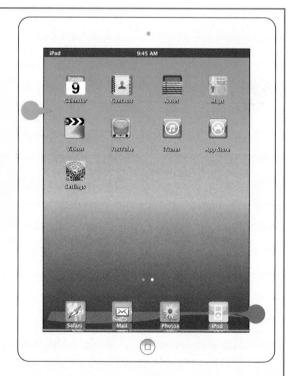

App Icons

The icons located on the Home screen represent the apps installed on the iPad. The apps that come preinstalled on the iPad cannot be deleted. You can only move them. Each time you download a new app from the App Store, a new icon appears on the Home screen, which you can move or delete/uninstall. Press your finger on the app that you want to move until the icons start to wiggle. You can then drag the icon to a new location or you can tap the ⊗ to delete it.

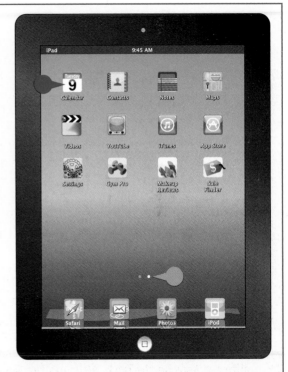

Pages

Located at the bottom of the Home screen, just above the Dock, are multiple small dots signifying that more screens are located on the desktop. You can navigate between these pages by sliding the touch screen to either the left or right with your finger. You can also tap a dot to move forward or backward through pages. Initially, there are only two dots: the Home screen (right) and Spotlight (left). Each time that you fill up an entire page with app icons, a new page is created. You can also drag an existing icon off-screen to manually create new pages. The dot for the current page is filled with white.

Explore Important iPad Settings

Your iPad is a versatile device that provides you with many options for customization, including accessibility options and parental controls. You can configure your iPad to give verbal cues for those who are hearing impaired and make text larger to accommodate the visually impaired.

If children use your iPad or have an iPad of their own, you can keep them from viewing or purchasing questionable material on the Internet by setting universal parental controls. For a clean start, you can choose to restore your iPad to its default presets. Understanding your iPad's settings can help you get the most from your iPad.

Learn about Accessibility Options

The iPad possesses features that make it more accommodating for people who may be visually impaired, hard of hearing, or deaf, or who have a physical or learning disability. The iPad is equipped with a screen reader and support for the playback of closed-captioned content and other helpful universal access features.

Explore Parental Controls

If children have access to your iPad or if they have one of their own, the iPad has parental control features that can help you restrict the content they are exposed to on the web. You can restrict their access to popular social networking sites, such as YouTube, and even restrict their downloading capabilities from the App Store and iTunes.

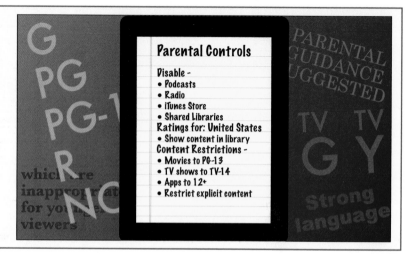

Learn about Airplane Mode

While on a plane, you must deactivate any device that may receive phone calls, wireless messaging, and Internet access. When you travel, you can place the iPad into Airplane mode, which disables its wireless abilities, therefore making it an approved device while in flight. While in Airplane mode, you can enjoy previously downloaded content, such as music, videos, and eBooks, during your flight. Airplane mode is now available on both the 3G and Wi-Fi models.

Restore iPad Default Presets

If you have spent a lot of time configuring your iPad and would like to return it to its previous state, such as when you first purchased it, you can always reset it to the default settings. If you ever want to sell your iPad, consider resetting the iPad so no one has access to your personal data, such as your contacts, emails, and appointments. You can choose to erase all content and settings when you reset the iPad. See Chapter 2 for more on resetting your iPad.

Find My iPad

Out of the many places that you may take your iPad, it is quite possible that you could leave or misplace your iPad. You can download a free app from the App Store to your iPhone, Mac or PC named Find My iPad that can help you locate your iPad on a map using GPS. You can also set the Find My iPad app to play a sound that you can use to help locate your iPad or display a message on the screen with your contact information.

CHAPTER 2

Configure the iPad

Your iPad is a state-of-the-art entertainment system and productivity tool that can be customized to fit your own specific needs. In this chapter, you discover the variety of settings at your disposal to personalize your iPad and how to optimize them for your everyday life. You learn how to not only customize its appearance but also its functionality, including security settings and parental controls.

Customize the Home Screen

The Home screen is where you start many of the activities on your iPad. As you purchase new apps for your iPad, the number of icons on the Home screen multiplies, which may prompt you to rearrange some of them. You can move similarly themed apps to a different page, put them in a folder, delete apps you have downloaded, or limit the number of apps per page to make them more easily searchable.

You have the ability to rearrange the order of apps located in the Dock at the bottom of the screen. The items in the Dock remain the same across all screens, providing you easy access to core apps. One of the most basic ways to customize your iPad is to rearrange the icons on the screen to your liking.

Customize the Home Screen

1 Display any page of the iPad Home screen.

Note: You can achieve this by closing out of whatever app you may currently be in by pressing the **Home** button (▢).

Note: This example uses the second iPad screen, which includes downloaded apps.

2 Tap and hold any of the app icons on the Home screen and continue to press until the icons begin to wiggle.

Note: When the icons begin to wiggle, you can move them around with your finger.

③ Tap and drag the icon that you want to move to a new location.

Note: The surrounding icons move and adjust around the placement of the icon you drag.

Note: You can even drag the icon off the screen, to the right, to create a new page.

④ Press the **Home** button (▭).

Your iPad saves the current icon arrangement.

TIPS

Can I move icons located on the Dock at the bottom of the screen?

Yes. You can press one of the icons on the Dock, and when it starts to wiggle, rearrange it on the Dock. You can even remove it from the Dock and replace it with another icon, or simply add more apps to the Dock, up to a maximum of six.

Can I delete icons from the Home screen?

You can delete icons that you have downloaded and installed on your iPad. When the icons begin to wiggle, an x (⊗) appears in the top left corner of the icon. You can tap the ⊗ to remove the icon and uninstall the app. Over time, if you find that you do not use certain apps very often, consider moving them to another page or delete them. You cannot delete the preinstalled apps.

Reset the Default Home Screen Layout

Your iPad is a fully customizable device. Each iPad owner's Home screen layout can be as unique as the owner herself. You can change the wallpaper, add extra Home screens, rearrange icons, and delete downloaded apps when needed. Over time, what you need in a Home screen layout can change.

After you have experimented with many different arrangements, you may want to return the Home screen to the default layout. Any preinstalled apps that you had rearranged on your device return to their original location. Your iPad makes it easy for you to reset the changes you have made for a fresh new start.

Reset the Default Home Screen Layout

1 Display the Home screen.

Note: You can achieve this by exiting whatever app you may currently be in by pressing the **Home** button (⬚).

2 Tap **Settings**.

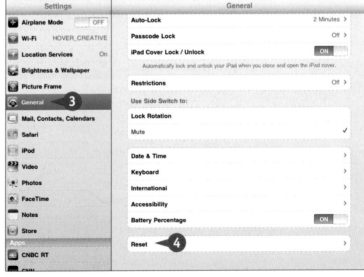

The Settings screen appears.

3 Tap **General**.

4 Tap **Reset**.

The Reset screen appears.

⑤ Tap **Reset Home Screen Layout**.

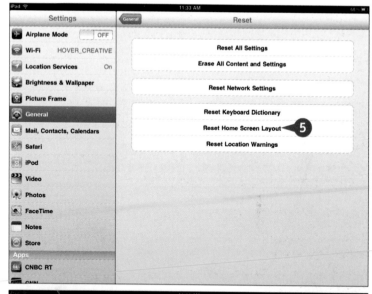

A dialog warns you that the Home screen will be reset to the factory default layout.

⑥ Tap **Reset**.

iPad resets the Home screen to the factory default layout.

TIP

Is my new app deleted when I reset the Home screen?
No. Resetting the Home screen does not discard any new app you may have added to the Home screen. Only the layout is affected. For example, if you have previously moved the Notes app icon to another page, the icon is placed back on the first page in its original location. If you moved one of the default app icons from the Dock, the icon is placed back on the Dock once you reset the Home screen layout.

Protect Your iPad with a Passcode

By default, your iPad is set to lock after a period of inactivity. This protects your iPad from accidental taps while it is in your bag or carried in your hands. Unfortunately, locking your iPad does not protect confidential information that may be on it. When you lay your iPad down, anyone so inclined can unlock it and view your personal information. To keep your sensitive materials private, you can protect your iPad with a four-digit passcode. Remembering your passcode is highly important. If you forget your passcode, you will have to restore your iPad software.

Protect Your iPad with a Passcode

1 Tap **Settings** on the Home screen.

The Settings screen appears.

2 Tap **General**.

The General screen appears.

3 Tap **Passcode Lock**.

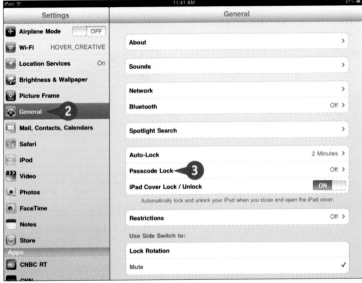

The Passcode Lock screen appears.

④ Tap **Turn Passcode On**.

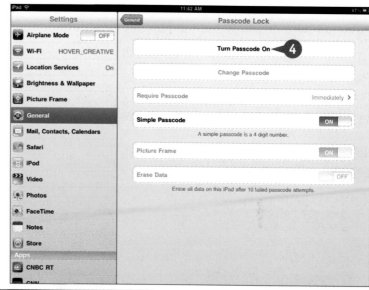

The Set Passcode dialog opens.

⑤ Type your passcode.

iPad prompts you to type the code again.

Note: For security purposes, the code you type is represented in the box with dots.

⑥ Type the passcode again.

The code is now saved, and the Passcode Lock screen appears.

Note: You can tap **Require Passcode** on the Passcode Lock screen to specify how much time elapses before your iPad locks and requests the passcode.

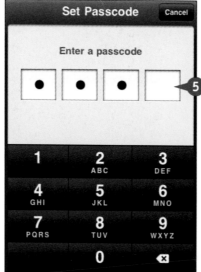

TIPS

How do I change my passcode?
You can change your passcode from the Passcode Lock screen. You need to know the original code to change it to a new one. Tap **Change Passcode**. Tap **Settings** on the Home screen, and then tap **General**. Tap **Change Passcode Lock**, and then type the old passcode. Type a new passcode.

How do I turn off my passcode?
You can turn off your passcode from the Passcode Lock screen. Tap **Turn Passcode Off**, and then type the current passcode to deactivate it.

Configure the iPad Sleep Setting

You can manually put your iPad into Sleep mode by pressing the Sleep/Wake button located on the top right side on the device. During periods of inactivity, your iPad automatically goes into Sleep mode and locks as a means of conserving battery power and protecting against unwanted taps. You can specify the amount of time that elapses before the iPad goes to sleep.

If the default time of 2 minutes is too short, you can change it to a longer time of 5 minutes, 10 minutes, 15 minutes, or Never. Experiment with these settings to see which works best for you.

Configure the iPad Sleep Setting

① Tap **Settings** on the Home screen.

The Settings screen appears.

② Tap **General**.

The General screen appears.

③ Tap **Auto-Lock**.

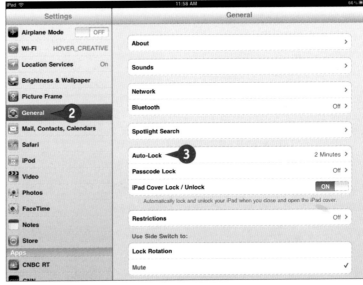

The Auto-Lock screen appears.

④ Tap the interval that you want.

Note: Your choices are 2 Minutes, 5 Minutes, 10 Minutes, 15 Minutes, and Never.

iPad saves the new interval.

● The current interval appears with a check mark.

⑤ Tap **General** to return to the General settings screen.

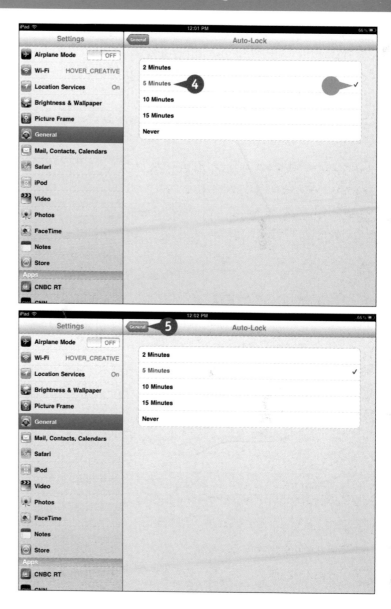

Anything else I should know about iPad sleep settings?

You should know that you do not have to wait for the iPad to fall asleep on its own; you can manually put your iPad in Sleep mode by pressing the Sleep/Wake button. If you use a Smart Cover with your iPad 2, you can put your iPad 2 into Sleep mode just by closing the cover. Consider putting the iPad into Sleep mode after you have finished using it to help conserve battery power. Every little precaution you can take to conserve battery power does have an impact on battery life.

Turn Sounds On and Off

You can disable all sound on your iPad 2 in three ways. You can use the Volume Up/Down button located on the right side of your iPad in portrait orientation. You can use the quickest option of toggling the Silent/Screen Rotation lock located just above the Up/Down button. The third option is to go into the settings and disable sounds.

The advantage of disabling sound from the Settings menu is that you can pick and choose which sounds to disable. Consider turning off the sounds if you will use your iPad in a meeting where beeps and clicks may be deemed distracting or altogether inappropriate.

Turn Sounds On and Off

1 Tap **General** in the Settings menu.

2 Tap **Sounds**.

The Sounds screen appears.

3 Tap the sounds that you do not want to the **Off** position.

When you tap **New Mail** to **Off**, the chime you hear when you receive an email is deactivated.

When you tap **Sent Mail** to **Off**, the swoosh that you hear when you send an email is deactivated.

When you tap **Calendar Alerts** to **Off**, the chime that you hear whenever you receive an event alert is deactivated.

When you tap **Lock Sounds** to **Off**, the click your iPad makes when you lock and use the Slide to Unlock button is deactivated.

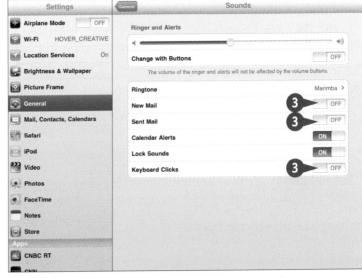

Set the Silent/Screen Rotation Lock Switch

When the original iPad was first introduced in 2010, it was showcased with a hardware switch labeled as a Mute switch. Just before the launch of the device, Apple revealed a minor tweak to this switch and changed it to a Screen Rotation lock. In the update to iOS 4.2 beta, Apple changed the switch back to a mute option. By popular demand, iOS 4.3 gives you the option of both a mute option and a screen rotation lock. You can configure this switch under Settings or in the task switcher.

Configuring the switch as a Screen Rotation lock helps prevent the iPad from switching orientation as you move it in the act of reading an eBook, browsing the web, or other tasks.

Set the Silent/Screen Rotation Lock Switch

1 Tap **Settings** on the Home screen.

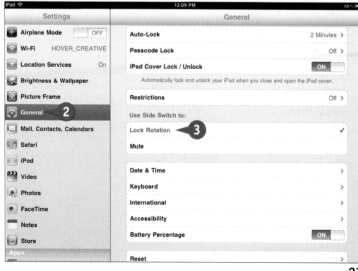

The Settings screen appears.

2 Tap **General**.

The General screen appears.

3 Tap **Lock Rotation** in the Use Side Switch to options.

Your iPad's Silent/Screen Rotation lock has been set to lock the current screen orientation, when used.

Note: You can lock rotation if you have the switch set to Mute or vice versa from within the task switcher. Hold the iPad in the orientation you want locked, and then press the Home button twice. Swipe left to right in the task switcher that appears at the bottom of the screen. Tap the **Orientation Lock** button (🔄) to lock the iPad in the current orientation.

Adjust the Brightness of the Screen

Your iPad is equipped with sensors that enable it to automatically adjust the brightness of the screen according to ambient light. This feature is called Auto-Brightness. If the ambient light is dim, iPad automatically brightens the screen. If the ambient light is bright, the iPad screen dims. This is a hands-free way to find a balance between battery life and screen brightness.

You can also manually adjust the screen brightness of your iPad to your own liking within the Settings menu. Apps such as iBooks also include features that allow you to adjust the brightness of the screen without leaving the program.

Adjust the Brightness of the Screen

① Tap **Brightness & Wallpaper**.

The Brightness & Wallpaper screen appears.

② Drag the **Brightness** slider to dim or brighten the screen.

Note: Dragging the **Brightness** slider to the left dims the screen. Dragging the **Brightness** slider to the right brightens the screen.

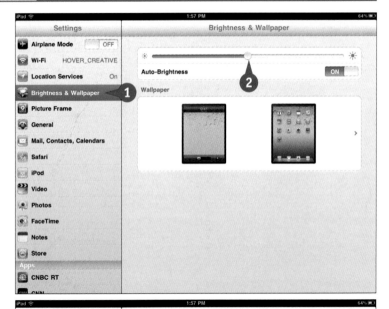

③ Tap the **Auto-Brightness** setting to the **Off** position.

iPad saves your new brightness settings.

Note: If you do not turn off Auto-Brightness, iPad does not maintain your new brightness settings. It continues to adjust automatically when the ambient light changes.

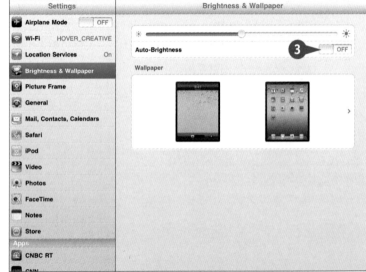

Switch to Airplane Mode

When traveling on an airplane, you can place your iPad into Airplane mode, which disables any wireless features that may interfere with the operation of aircraft instruments. Airplane mode is now a feature offered for all iPad models. While in Airplane mode and when the Wi-Fi has been deactivated, you can still enjoy downloaded content, such as music, videos, and eBooks.

Some airlines allow you to turn on Wi-Fi after the aircraft has reached a specified altitude. Knowing how to switch to Airplane mode allows you to comply with airline regulations. Learning how to turn off and on Wi-Fi enables you to enjoy wireless features where allowed.

Switch to Airplane Mode

1 Tap **Settings**.

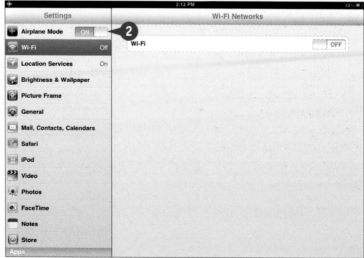

The Settings open.

2 Tap **Airplane Mode** to the **On** position in the Settings menu.

Your iPad's wireless capabilities have been deactivated.

Note: You can tap **Wi-Fi** in Settings, and then tap the **Wi-Fi** setting to the **On** position where permitted.

Change the iPad Wallpaper

Perhaps the most basic customization you can perform with your iPad is changing the default wallpaper for the Home screen. The iPad has several Apple-designed wallpapers from which to choose, but you can personalize your screen by choosing one of your own. Your iPad 2 is capable of capturing images that you can use as wallpapers. You can sync photos captured with a higher-quality camera from your computer or transfer them with the iPad Camera Connection Kit.

There are many apps that you can download in the App Store, such as Wallpapers, where you can browse and download popular wallpaper art for your iPad. Changing your wallpaper enables you to customize the look of your iPad.

Change the iPad Wallpaper

1 Tap **Brightness & Wallpaper** in the Settings menu.

2 Tap in the **Wallpaper** field.

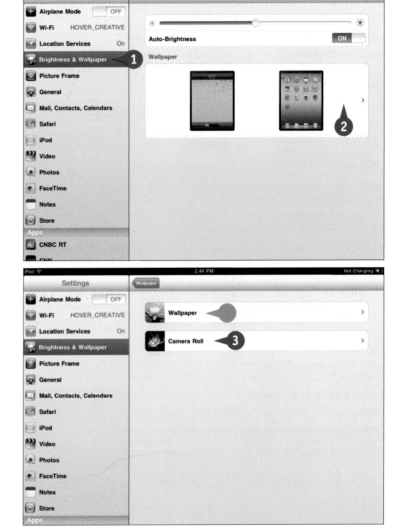

The photo collections on your iPad appear.

3 Tap the collection of photos from which you want to choose.

● At this point, by tapping **Wallpaper**, you can choose pre-existing wallpaper designed by Apple or you can choose one of your own photos.

④ Tap the image you want to use.

The Move and Scale screen appears.

⑤ Position the image with your finger until the image is situated the way you want it to appear.

The photo is repositioned.

Note: Start with your fingers pinched and then open your fingers to enlarge the scale of the image. Decrease the enlarged image by pinching your fingers closed on the screen.

The scale of the photo is adjusted.

⑥ Tap **Set Both**.

The image is set as the wallpaper for both the Lock screen and the Home screen.

● You can choose to make the picture the wallpaper for either the Lock screen or the Home screen. You can use a different image for each if you want.

TIP

How do I get my own photographs onto my iPad?
You have the ability to capture photographs straight from your iPad 2 using the front and back cameras. You can also connect your iPad to your computer and sync the photographs that you have in iPhoto or Photoshop Elements to your iPad, or you can use the iPad Camera Connection Kit. The camera connection kit provides you with two ways of getting your photos onto your iPad. You can either attach your camera to the iPad with a USB cable or insert a memory card directly into the connector to transfer your photos. The camera connection kit is sold separately.

Configure Parental Controls

The iPad has parental control features that can help you restrict the content that children using either your iPad or their own are exposed to on the web. You can restrict their access to popular online communities, such as YouTube, and even restrict downloading from the App Store and iTunes. You can also restrict their participation in multiplayer games found in Game Center and their ability to add friends.

It is important to understand that when you enable parental controls for your iPad, the restrictions are universal. Anyone who uses your iPad must abide by the set restrictions, unless they have access to the passcode.

Configure Parental Controls

1 Tap **General** in the Settings menu.

The General screen appears.

2 Tap **Restrictions**.

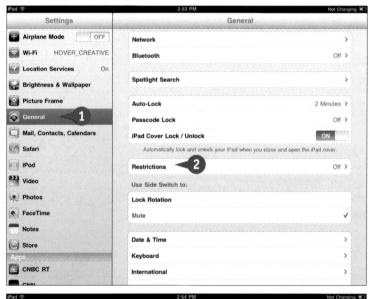

The Restrictions screen appears.

3 Tap **Enable Restrictions**.

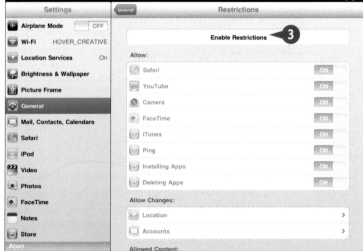

iPad displays the Set Passcode screen so you can specify a four-digit code to use to override the parental controls.

Note: This passcode is not the same passcode used to password-protect access to your iPad.

④ Type the four-digit restriction passcode.

iPad prompts you to type the passcode again.

⑤ Type the four-digit restriction passcode again.

iPad returns you to the Restrictions screen and enables all controls.

⑥ Tap each setting to **On** or **Off** to enable or disable restrictions.

The restrictions are enabled.

● You can tap the **In-App Purchases** setting to **Off** if you want to restrict children from making purchases within apps such as iTunes.

Note: The Ratings For setting lets you set restrictions by using a specified country's rating system for Music, Podcasts, Movies, TV Shows, and Apps. For example, the rating PG applies to movies in the United States.

Note: You can tap a category, such as Music & Podcasts, Movies, TV Shows, and Apps, and then choose the highest rating (G, PG, PG 13, R, or NC-17) you will allow for your children.

⑦ Tap **General** to return to the General settings screen.

TIPS

How do I turn off the restrictions?
Turning off the restrictions requires that you know your passcode. Tap **Disable Restrictions** on the Restrictions screen. Enter the passcode again to disable the restrictions.

What if I forget my passcode?
You will have to connect your iPad to your computer and then restore your iPad software from iTunes.

Reset the iPad

Over time and after many different configurations, you may want to clear all or some of your iPad's settings and then return the iPad to the default settings. Your iPad conveniently gives you options for what you may choose to reset, including these options: Reset Network Settings, Reset Keyboard Dictionary, and Reset Home Screen Layout. Resetting your iPad not only gives you a fresh start at configuring your iPad, but it could also help resolve issues if something is not working right. You can reset your iPad as a last resort for fixing an issue if other troubleshooting measures have failed.

Reset the iPad

① Tap **Settings** on the Home screen.

The Settings screen appears.

② Tap **General**.

The General screen appears.

③ Tap **Reset**.

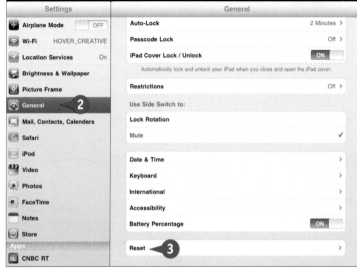

The Reset screen appears.

④ Tap the Reset option you want.

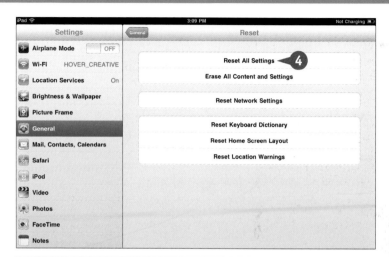

A dialog opens, notifying you that all settings will be reset.

⑤ Tap **Reset**.

The settings you have specified are reset.

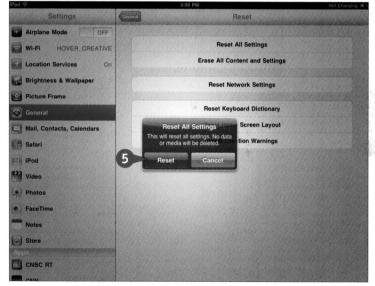

TIP

What does each of the reset options do?
The reset options available are as follows:

• **Reset All Settings**: Custom settings revert back to the factory default settings.

• **Erase All Content and Settings**: Custom settings are reset, and all data on your iPad is removed. You should use this option before gifting or selling your iPad.

• **Reset Network Settings**: Wi-Fi network settings are deleted.

• **Reset Keyboard Dictionary**: A list of all the keyboard recommendations you have rejected are cleared.

• **Reset Home Screen Layout**: This returns the Home screen icons to their default arrangements.

• **Reset Location Warnings**: This clears location preferences for your apps.

Cut, Copy, and Paste Text

Your iPad makes it easy for you to transfer data such as editable and noneditable text by copying or cutting it and pasting it in a new location. Editable text includes text found in emails or in an editable document such in Pages. An example of noneditable text would be text found on a website.

The ability to cut, copy, and paste comes in handy if you should ever find a block of text on a web page that you want to share with friends or family. You can copy the paragraph and then paste it into an email message. The procedure differs depending on if the text is editable or noneditable.

Cut, Copy, and Paste Text

Select and Copy Noneditable Text

Note: An example of noneditable text would be text found on a website.

1 Tap and hold in the section of the noneditable text that you want to copy.

A selection box with handles appears around the text. A button allowing you to copy the text also appears.

2 Drag the handles of the selection box around the text that you want.

3 Tap **Copy**.

The text is placed on the Clipboard, which you do not see, but it is there.

Select and Copy Editable Text

Note: An example of editable text would be a URL for a website or the body of an email message.

1 Tap and hold until you see the magnifying glass and then release.

Two buttons appear, providing you with options.

2 Tap one of the options.

Note: Tap **Select** if you want to select only part of the text, or tap **Select All** to select all the text.

Note: In this example, Select was chosen.

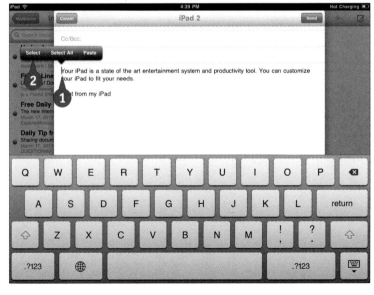

Part of the text is highlighted in blue and two more options appear, asking what you want to do with the text.

③ Tap and drag the selection handles around the text that you want.

④ Tap the option you want.

Note: Copy was chosen for this example.

⑤ Open the app in which you want to paste the text.

Note: In this example, text was pasted into a new email message.

⑥ Tap where you want to paste the text.

⑦ Tap **Paste**.

iPad adds the copied text to the email.

Copy and Paste a Photo

Occasionally, you may encounter a picture online that you just have to share with someone else. Your iPad makes it easy for you to copy and paste photos to a new location. Similarly, you may encounter a picture online or from your own personal website that you just have to share with someone else. Instead of emailing a link to the page, just send the picture to a friend along with a comment.

The ability to copy and paste photos is a great convenience. The process is very similar to copying and pasting noneditable text. Do be aware of copyright issues before copying images from random websites and using them commercially.

Copy and Paste a Photo

1 Tap and hold the image you want to copy.

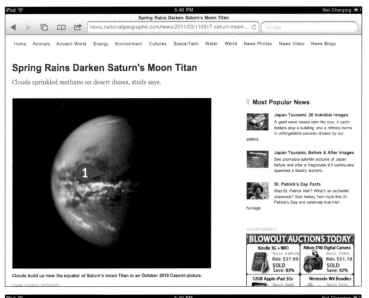

A pop-up menu of image options appears.

2 Tap **Copy**.

The photo is copied into your iPad's memory.

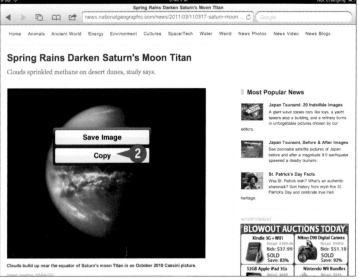

③ Open the app into which you want to paste the photo.

Note: This example pastes the photo into an email message.

④ Tap where you want the image to appear.

Options appear, asking you what you want to do.

⑤ Tap **Paste**.

iPad pastes the photo.

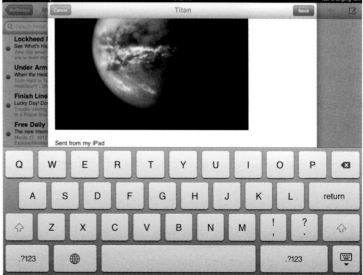

Search Your iPad by Using Spotlight

The more that you use your iPad for work or for play, the more content you accumulate over time. Although the iPad does not have a large hard drive like a computer, it is still capable of amassing plenty of content. After a while, locating your content can become difficult. Spotlight is a simple search box that enables you to search your entire iPad for content.

From your main/first home page, click the Home button once to access Spotlight. Spotlight is a helpful tool for you to find content for which you do not know the exact location.

Search Your iPad by Using Spotlight

1 Tap the **Home** button (▢) to return to the Home screen.

2 Tap ▢ again to display the Spotlight screen.

Note: From the Home screen, you could have also flicked to the right to access the Spotlight screen.

③ Type the search text.

Items that match your search begin to appear on-screen.

④ Tap **Search**.

The complete search results appear.

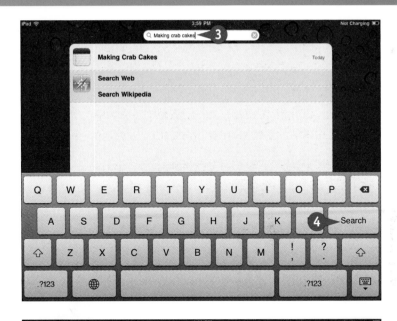

⑤ Tap the item you were looking for.

The item opens.

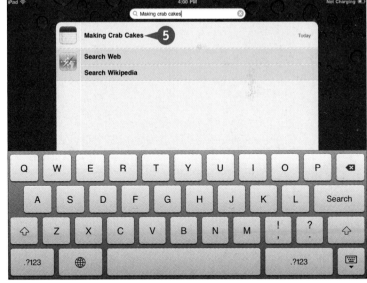

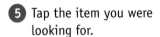

TIP

Where exactly can you search with Spotlight?

Spotlight searches your entire iPad, including apps. Spotlight has the ability to search many apps on your iPad, including Mail, Contacts, Notes, iPod, and Calendar. You can use the Search field to search an individual app installed on your iPad or all of them simultaneously. Tap any of the app icons that appear in your search to open the app. You can configure Spotlight searches in Settings under the General options.

CHAPTER 3

Get the Most Out of the Internet

Your iPad offers many great features for experiencing the Internet. The Safari web browser provides you with many options for optimizing your web-browsing experience. In this chapter, you learn the basics of Internet access, Wi-Fi networks, and 3G service.

The Safari options appear.

3 Tap **Search Engine**.

The Search Engine screen appears.

Note: The current default search has a check mark next to it.

4 Tap **Bing**.

● iPad places a check mark next to the Bing option and makes Bing your default search engine.

Is there any way that I can set my default web page to a site other than Google, Yahoo!, or Bing?
No. Unlike with your computer, you cannot set the default web page to whatever you want — for example, your favorite online news source. Your only choices are Google and Yahoo. With that being said, Safari opens to whatever page you had visited last. Before you leave Safari, you could make sure you return to the page you want it to open to. It is not an automatic fix, but at least Safari opens with the page you want.

Manage Multiple Web Pages

i̇Pad was designed to be intuitive, easy to use, and efficient. Browsing the web just got faster with the iPad 2. Web pages load and reload faster than ever with the Nitro JavaScript engine and the faster dual-core A5 processor. If you like to multitask, iPad makes it easy for you to open multiple web browser screens at the same time, load different pages into them, and navigate between the multiple pages.

You can view multiple open pages in a grid, enabling you to move quickly between pages with just the tap of your fingers. The ability to manage multiple browser pages enables you to perform multiple searches.

Manage Multiple Web Pages

① Tap **Safari** on the Home screen.

Safari opens.

② Tap the **Pages** icon (⬚) on the menu bar.

Safari displays a new blank page, along with the current page as a thumbnail.

③ Tap **New Page**.

The new page opens full screen, along with the on-screen keyboard. A blinking cursor appears in the Search field.

Note: You can hold your finger on a link within a page and then choose **Open in New Page** to open that link in a new Safari window.

④ Load a new website.

Note: You can do this by typing a web address, typing a search, or even tapping a bookmark.

⑤ Repeat steps **1** to **4** for additional pages if needed.

Note: When scrolling on any web page, you can double-tap the top of the iPad screen to automatically return to the top of the web page.

● You can clear your web browsing history by tapping the **Bookmarks** icon (📖) and then tapping **History**. Tap **Clear History**.

TIP

Any tips on navigating between multiple pages?

Yes. Your iPad can have up to nine web pages open at the same time. You can tap the **Pages** icon (▢) on the menu bar to see all the pages at once in thumbnails. You can navigate between the pages you have open in this view, and you can also tap the ⊗ located in the upper left corner of the web page thumbnail to delete pages you no longer need.

Explore Browser Security and Privacy Options

Regardless of what browser you may be using, Internet criminals are hard at work trying to collect your personal information. When you surf the Internet, you open your iPad up to security risks that can compromise your privacy. If something looks suspicious, use common sense. Do not hand over your personal information without vetting the source. Become well acquainted with the browser security and privacy options of your iPad.

Learning about browser security options can help you protect your iPad from security risks on the Internet. The security options for your iPad are located in Safari under Settings.

Explore Fraud Warning

Fraudulent websites designed to appear as legitimate companies can pose real threats to your privacy. The hook that many of these frauds use is to send you an email that requests you to update your account information on their site. The email can appear from a reputable company of which you may actually have an account, such as eBay. The scheme is to get you to hand over your personal information. Once it has your information, an experienced criminal can easily steal your identity. You should turn on Fraud Warning so Safari can warn you about the suspect page and not load the website.

Understand JavaScript

JavaScript is a scripting language that exists within the HTML for a web page and is used for such things as rollovers. JavaScript can also be used for foul purposes by those who are inclined to do so. By default, your iPad is set to support JavaScript. You can turn JavaScript support off if you choose to visit a suspect website. Keep in mind that most web pages do not work without JavaScript, so you should not turn it off permanently.

Understand Pop-Up Blocking

Pop-up ads are a form of aggressive online advertising, often used to attract traffic to a certain site. Pop-ups get their name from their actions. A site that you are viewing may open a new web browser page and load an advertisement into it, which can be annoying. By default, your iPad is configured to block pop-ups. It is important to note here that pop-ups

can serve legitimate purposes, such as login pages, media players, and announcements. When navigating certain websites, you may need to set the Block Pop-ups option to Off.

Explore Cookies

Cookies are small text files that some websites store on your iPad to track your website activity. One common use of them is for online shopping sites to record your personal information and track your shopping cart. On the more annoying end, when you visit some websites, the server can store one of these text files on your computer as a means to track your movements and display advertisements personalized for your viewing habits. By default, your iPad is set to accept cookies only from sites that you visit and rejects all third-party cookies. You can also configure your iPad to Never accept cookies or Always accept cookies. The default option of From visited is the better option of these three.

Clear the Browser History and the Cache

Behind the scenes, Safari secretly records the places you have visited on the web, known as *History*. History is a great feature if you need to retrace your steps to find a website for which you may have forgotten the name. The contents of the pages you have visited are stored in what is called the *browser cache*. The information stored in the browser cache enables websites to

load faster when you visit them. Your iPad gives you the ability to clear the History of the web pages you have visited. You can also clear the cache to try to solve loading issues that may occur.

Bookmark Your Favorite Websites

When you are surfing the Internet, your iPad makes it easy for you to save your favorite websites as bookmarks so that you can quickly return to them later. Adding a bookmark for a website enables you to skip the process of typing a web address to revisit the page.

Over time, you can accumulate a large number of bookmarks. It is very important that you supply descriptive names for each bookmark to help you manage your large collection. Bookmarked web pages appear in a list, and all you have to do is tap the bookmark to visit the page.

Bookmark Your Favorite Websites

1 Navigate to the website that you want to save.

Note: You can do this by typing the web address or typing in the search field and tapping and choosing an option from the search list.

Note: You can save time typing web addresses. When typing in the address field, hold your finger down on the .com button on the keyboard to reveal the hidden .net, .org, .us, and .edu.

2 Tap the **Share** icon ( ) on the address bar.

A menu appears, presenting you with options for the website.

Note: You can add a web page icon to the Home screen for a page you frequently visit. Tap the icon and the page opens.

3 Tap **Add Bookmark**.

A blinking cursor appears in the address field.

④ Type a new name for the page if needed.

● The address for the website appears beneath the name field.

⑤ Tap **Save**.

By default, your iPad saves the website at the top level of the Bookmarks list.

Note: For faster access, you can make your bookmarks visible at the top of your browser. Go to Safari in the Settings and set **Always Show Bookmarks Bar** to **On**.

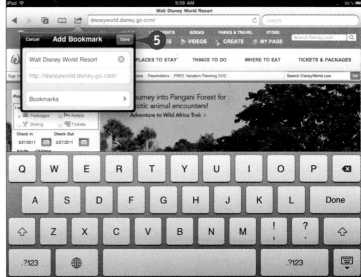

TIPS

Can I sync bookmarks on my computer with my iPad?

Yes. If you have a Mac or a PC, you can sync the bookmarks with the Safari web browser on your Mac and the Internet Explorer or Safari browser on your PC with your iPad. You can also sync bookmarks with MobileMe.

Can I edit the bookmarks on my iPad?

Yes. You can tap the **Share** icon () on the main menu bar and tap a bookmark or folder that contains the bookmark you want to edit. You can create new bookmark folders, delete bookmark folders, reposition a bookmark or folder by dragging, and edit the name of a bookmark or web address.

Explore Touch-Screen Navigation Tips

Your iPad places the power of the Internet and many entertainment and productive software apps at your fingertips — literally. Now Apple has given you even more control over how you navigate your iPad. iOS 4.3 now supports four- and five-finger multi-touch gestures. To enable these four- and five-finger gestures on your iPad, you must download and install the Xcode 4 developer toolset from the App store onto your iPad. You are given the option to toggle these new gestures between the On and Off positions in the Settings. If you are used to navigating websites and apps with your iPhone or iPod touch, then you are familiar with zooming, scrolling, and turning pages with your fingers.

Switch between Open Apps — Four Fingers

iOS 4.3 supplies you more options for navigating between open apps on your iPad. You no longer have to access the multi-tasking bar to switch between running apps. iOS 4.3 supports a four-finger gesture that enables you to flick through running apps at full screen. For example, suppose that you have Safari, Settings, and Maps running simultaneously. You can press four fingers on the display and flick right to left or left to right to switch from each app. Some apps may take more time than others to load as you switch.

Five-Finger Gestures

iOS 4.3 supports five-finger multi-touch gestures. Now your fingers do not have to leave the screen to press the Home button to close an app and return to a Home screen. Touch four or five fingers to the screen displaying an open app, and then pinch your fingers to close the app and return to the Home screen. If you want to access the multi-tasking bar, swipe up from the bottom of the screen with four or five fingers to reveal it at the bottom of the screen. iPad 2 moves a step closer to complete virtual control.

Scroll and Zoom

Scrolling web pages and zooming into a specific area on a website are common practices. You can scroll up and down web pages with a flick of your finger. To get a closer look at a graphic on a page, place your thumb and forefinger on the screen, pinch them closely, and then move them apart to zoom into an image. To zoom out of the image, place your two fingers apart on the screen and then pinch them closed. You do not have to be exact when returning the page to its previous scale. Just pinch your fingers closed, and iPad snaps the page back to the default scale.

One Tap

A single tap with one finger is perhaps the most used navigation method on the touch screen. You can tap a link to open a new web page, tap in an online form to receive a blinking cursor, and tap to make the on-screen keyboard appear so you can begin typing. If you are reading down a long web page and want to return to the top of the page, you can tap on the menu bar area, and iPad returns you to the top of the page.

Double-Tap

Double-tapping is a quick way to zoom into pages. For example, if you are reading text, a chart, or a table that is particularly small, you can double-tap to magnify the page. To magnify a specific area of the page, just double-tap on top of that specific area to magnify it. To return the page to its original scale, just double-tap the page again.

Tap, Hold, and Drag

Tapping and then holding and dragging can perform some very helpful functions on your iPad. On a Mac or Windows computer, you can hover the mouse cursor over a link on a web page to view the URL where the link will send you. You can do the same on your iPad by tapping and holding your finger on a link. You also receive a menu that gives you the options to Open, Open in New Page, and Copy. Tapping and holding on text highlights the text and gives you the option of copying the text. iPad highlights the area you want to copy in blue. You can drag the selection to encompass more text. If you tap in the white area between two paragraphs, your iPad highlights the entire body of text and gives you the option of copying it.

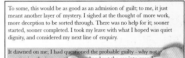

View in Landscape

The iPad also enables you to view websites and apps in various ways according to how you hold the iPad. For example, when using email, you hold the iPad in landscape orientation so you can view your email as a split screen, displaying both open email and messages in your Inbox. You can view an open email by itself by holding the iPad in portrait orientation. The iPad contains internal sensors that use gravity to sense the orientation of the device; thus, if the iPad is laying flat on a table and you rotate it, the orientation does not change.

Consider a Larger Keyboard

The iPad's on-screen keyboard provides you with the comfort of typing with an almost standard-sized keyboard. If the on-screen keyboard does not suffice for your practical everyday use, you can consider investing in a full-sized keyboard. The iPad Wireless Keyboard dock gives you the convenience of a full-sized keyboard along with the ergonomic and tactile experience you desire for more extensive writing tasks. A Bluetooth keyboard provides you with the flexibility of using a full-sized keyboard without a physical connection.

Turn On AutoFill

Safari has a preference that allows it to remember what info you type into online forms. This preference can come in handy if you commonly make purchases online. You may find yourself filling out form after form on your iPad, which may require you to fill in multiple fields of information, such as first and last name, mailing address, email address, and so on. You can turn on the AutoFill setting to help you fill out these forms faster by having your iPad automatically fill fields with information found in your Contacts list.

This could be a very practical preference for you considering that you may not always have the ergonomic benefits of using a full-sized keyboard with your iPad.

Turn On AutoFill

1 Tap **Settings** on the Home screen.

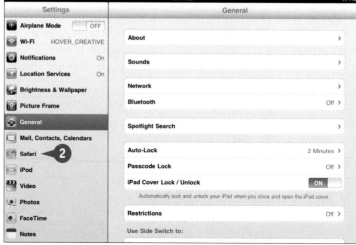

The Settings screen appears.

2 Tap **Safari**.

The Safari options appear.

③ Tap **AutoFill**.

The AutoFill screen appears.

④ Tap **Use Contact Info** to the **On** position.

The My Info field is now active.

⑤ Tap the **My Info** field.

A list of contacts located in your All Contacts list appears.

⑥ Tap the contact whose information you want iPad to use for autofill.

Note: This step requires that you have your own personal contact information in your All Contacts list.

The All Contacts list closes, and your iPad uses the information listed in the contact to automatically fill out forms.

TIP

How can I use the Names and Passwords option?
You can tap the **Names and Passwords** option to the **On** position so Safari remembers the names and passwords you have used on sites you have visited. When you return to these web pages, Safari automatically fills in this information in the proper fields for you. Be careful when using this feature, especially if more than one person uses your iPad. With Names and Passwords left On, someone can easily access your personal information when you supply that person with your password.

View an RSS Feed in Safari

If part of your daily routine includes reading news websites and blogs, accessing RSS feeds can help you streamline your efforts. Real Simple Syndication (RSS) feeds are special files that contain the most recent updated works on a website. There are also many RSS readers available in the App Store that can help you acquire and manage many RSS feeds. Some of them are free.

If your favorite blog does not post new content frequently but does so on an irregular basis, RSS feeds are a great way to receive the most recent posts displayed in your Safari web browser for your convenience. Not all blogs have RSS feeds.

View an RSS Feed in Safari

1 Tap **Safari** on the Home screen.

Safari opens.

2 Navigate to a site that you know has an RSS feed.

The site opens.

3 Locate the link to the RSS feed and then tap it.

Note: Look for an RSS icon () or a link that says View Feed XML or Subscribe.

4 Tap the link to the RSS feed.

The web-based RSS reader opens the feed.

Note: The most current posts are listed, of which you can tap and read the most recent articles.

TIPS

What is an efficient way to access my RSS feeds?
A great way to access RSS feeds is to bookmark them like you would any other site. Follow the steps in the section "Bookmark Your Favorite Websites" to bookmark your RSS feeds.

Can you recommend any good RSS apps that enable me to acquire and manage RSS feeds?
Yes. Pulse is a free RSS feed reader that enables you to acquire and manage multiple news feeds as an interactive mosaic. There are many other great options such as NewsRack.

Connect a Bluetooth Device with the iPad

In addition to the many other comforts and conveniences that iPad offers you, iPad also gives you the ability to connect to external devices wirelessly. Your iPad can interact with Bluetooth-enabled devices such as headphones, keyboards, and speakers. By default, Bluetooth is set to **Off** on your iPad. If you have already played with this setting, you can tell if Bluetooth is turned on by verifying that the Bluetooth symbol (■) can be seen in the status bar at the top of the screen.

Like most things iPad, connecting to a Bluetooth device has been made easy and can be accomplished in two phases: Discoverable and Pairing.

Connect a Bluetooth Device with the iPad

1 Make the device that you want to pair your iPad with discoverable.

Note: Bluetooth devices broadcast their availability only after you instruct them to. You may have to refer to your device's manual to discover how to do this.

2 Tap **Settings** on the Home screen.

The Settings screen appears.

3 Tap **General**.

The General options appear.

4 Tap **Bluetooth**.

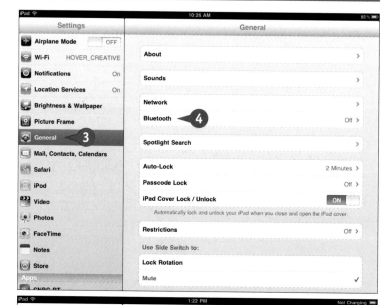

The Bluetooth options appear.

5 Tap **Bluetooth** into the **On** position.

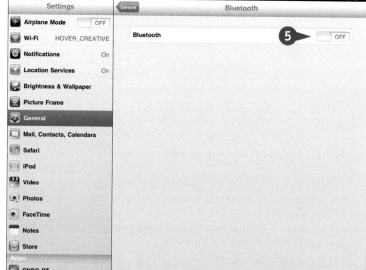

- The Bluetooth symbol (▮) appears in the status bar at the top of the screen.

  Discoverable devices appear in the Devices list.

6 Tap the device in the list that you want to pair with your iPad.

Note: Once a device is paired with your iPad, you never have to configure the device again.

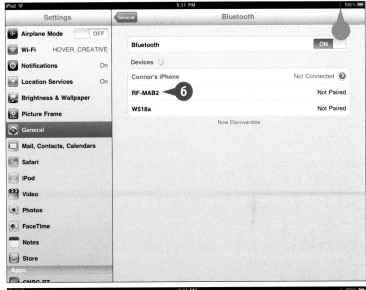

7 Type the password for the device, if prompted.

Note: You may have to refer to your device's manual to locate the password.

8 Tap **Pair**.

  You are now free to enjoy your wireless device.

Note: You can unpair a device by first selecting it in the Devices list, and then tapping **Unpair**.

Can I transfer files between my computer and my iPad via Bluetooth?
As of this publication, you cannot use Bluetooth to transfer files between your computer and your iPad. The iPad currently does not support any of the Bluetooth profiles or specifications to perform this.

What is the range of Bluetooth devices?
Bluetooth works up to a range of 30 feet. Once beyond 30 feet, device performance deteriorates.

CHAPTER 4

Maximize Email on the iPad

You can use your iPad's Mail app to send email and read email from friends, family, and colleagues. Your iPad makes it very easy for you to check email when you are on the go, supplying you with many of the same mail features you enjoy on your Mac or Windows computer. In this chapter, you learn how to set up an email account on your iPad as well as how to manage multiple email accounts and features.

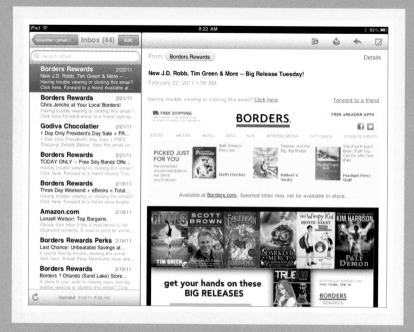

Learn about Managing Email Accounts

The iPad comes with a Mail app that is a scaled-back and streamlined version of what you may be accustomed to on a standard Mac. With that being said, the Mail app offers very effective features in managing your email while on the move. You can set up your iPad with one or more email accounts that you already use on your computer or iPhone, giving you quick and easy access.

The iPad recognizes five email services: Microsoft Exchange, MobileMe, Gmail, Yahoo! Mail, and AOL. You can also configure POP and IMAP accounts. By understanding email options with the iPad, you can best maximize your email experience.

Understand the Mail App

The Mail app on your iPad is a scaled-down but very capable version of the email program found on the Mac OS X operating system. The Mail app has been optimized for your iPad, providing you with features and settings that make it very convenient to use while you travel. You can configure your email to access accounts already set on your computer and even create accounts on the iPad itself.

Connect with Email Services

Out of the box, the iPad recognizes five email services: Microsoft Exchange, MobileMe, Google Gmail, Yahoo! Mail, and AOL. All you need to set up one of these accounts is the address and the account password. One of the most effective ways to use email on your iPad is to set up the Mail app to use an email account that you already use on your home computer. Syncing your iPad with your home computer enables you to check your email while traveling.

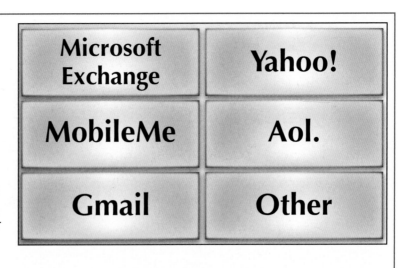

Set Up an iPad-Only Account

You can also set up a different account from the five email services your iPad recognizes. Your iPad also supports various email protocols, such as POP (Post Office Protocol) and IMAP (Internet Message Access Protocol). If you want to configure one of these protocols, you can ask your network administrator or email service provider what type of email account you currently have. This option takes considerably more work on your part, as opposed to simply syncing your Gmail or Yahoo! account.

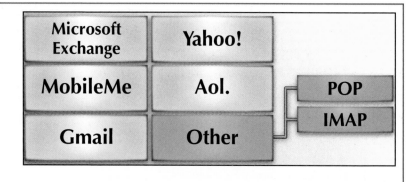

Specify the Default Email Account

Your iPad is capable of accessing multiple email accounts. You can specify which email account the Mail app opens when you tap the Mail app on the Home screen. When you specify a default email account, you are specifying the account from which a message is sent from another iPad app. For example, if you email a photo to someone from within the Photos app, it is sent via the default email account you have specified.

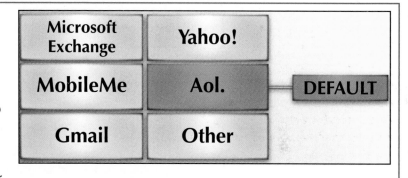

Switch, Disable, and Delete Accounts

After you have specified an email account as the default, you can easily switch to another account if needed. You can conserve your iPad's battery life by checking fewer email accounts. You can achieve this by temporarily disabling an account or by deleting an account. If one of your email accounts has become less relevant, you should consider deleting that account.

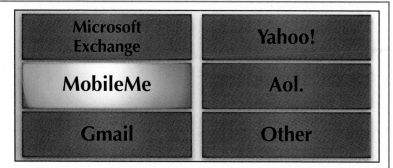

Add an Email Account for the First Time

E mail is a very simple and popular way to stay in contact with friends, family, and colleagues. One way to access email on your iPad is to set up the Mail app to connect to an email account already configured on your home computer. If you have set up an email account on your iPhone, then you are already familiar with the process.

The iPad recognizes five email services with a minimal amount of interaction on your behalf: Microsoft Exchange, MobileMe, Google Gmail, Yahoo! Mail, and AOL. Adding an email account enables you to check your most important email accounts while on the road.

Add an Email Account for the First Time

1 Tap **Mail** on the Home screen.

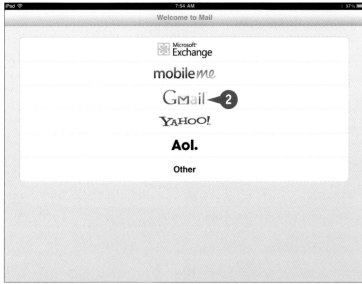

The Add Account screen appears.

Note: You can also access the Add Account screen by tapping **Settings** on the Home screen, tapping **Mail, Contacts, Calendars**, and then tapping **Add Account**.

2 Tap the name of the email service you are adding.

Note: This example uses Gmail.

The Add Account screen appears.

③ Tap the **Name** field and then type your name.

Note: This is the name shown when you exchange emails.

④ Tap the **Address** field and then type the address for the existing account.

⑤ Tap the **Password** field and then type the password for the existing account.

⑥ Tap the **Description** field and then type what kind of email account you are adding.

⑦ Tap **Next**.

The Verifying email account information screen appears.

If the information you provided was correct, you are taken to the next screen to specify if you want to sync Google Calendars and Notes on your iPad.

⑧ Tap **Save** to sync Google Calendars and Notes on your iPad.

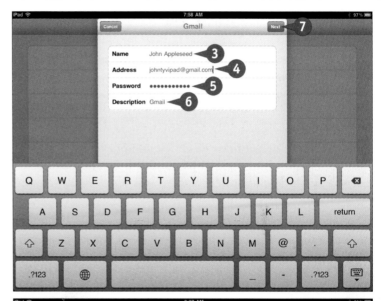

TIP

How do I add another email account after I have set up the first one?
You can add a second email account by following these steps. Tap **Settings** on the Home screen. Tap **Mail, Contacts, Calendars**. Your iPad displays the Mail, Contacts, Calendars screen. Tap **Add Account** to access the Add Account screen. Follow steps **2** to **7** to set up one of the five email services your iPad recognizes.

Create a New Email Account

You may find it necessary to create an email account that exists only on your iPad — perhaps for an iPad mailing list. Your iPad Mail app supports both the Post Office Protocol (POP) and Internet Message Access Protocol (IMAP) email account types. These types of accounts are what you receive through your Internet service provider (ISP), such as Comcast or Road Runner. You will need specific information for the new account, including the host name of the incoming and outgoing mail servers, to create a new email account on your iPad.

If your settings should fail to verify, double-check all the information. The majority of failures to verify come down to a single incorrect character entered.

Create a New Email Account

1 Tap **Mail, Contacts, Calendars** in the Settings menu.

Your iPad displays the Mail, Contacts, Calendars screen.

2 Tap **Add Account**.

The Add Account screen appears.

3 Tap **Other**.

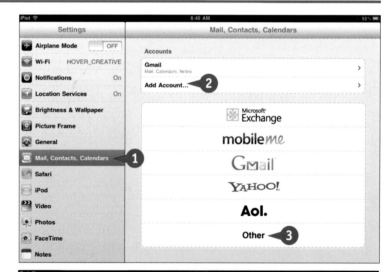

4 Tap **Add Mail Account**.

The New Account screen appears.

5 Tap the fields and then type the appropriate data into the **Name**, **Address**, **Password**, and **Description** fields.

6 Tap **Next**.

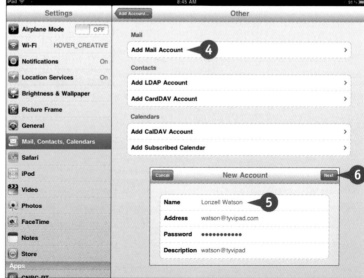

7 Tap the account type for the new email.

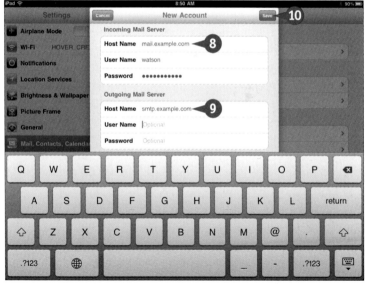

8 Type the host name, username, and password into the Incoming Mail Server section.

9 Type the host name, username, and password into the Outgoing Mail Server section.

Note: If your service provider requires a username and password, type those too.

10 Tap **Save**.

Your iPad verifies the account information and then returns you to the Mail Settings screen. The new account is added to the Accounts list.

TIPS

Which is the most popular account type?
POP is the most common. Incoming messages for an email account are temporarily stored on the provider's mail server. Typically, when you connect to the POP server, the email downloads to your device and is then removed from the server. By default, your iPad actually saves a copy on the server. IMAP works with your email messages only on the server. You will need to manage the contents of the server so you do not fill your storage quota. Once you fill your quota, you can no longer receive new mail until space has been freed.

What are the benefits of having your email stored only on the server?
When your email is stored on the server, you have the benefit of accessing those emails from multiple devices.

Specify the Default Email Account

O nce you have set up multiple email accounts, your iPad specifies one as the default. The default email account is the account in which a message is sent from within another app on your iPad. For example, if you tap the email address for a contact within the Contacts app, the message is sent from the default email account.

Specifying a different account does not dictate which mail account opens when you tap the Mail app on the Home screen. The email account that you used last opens when you access the mail app. Specifying a default email ensures that any email sent from another app on your iPad is sent from the designated account.

Specify the Default Email Account

1 Tap **Settings** on the Home screen.

The Settings screen appears.

2 Tap **Mail, Contacts, Calendars**.

Your iPad displays the Mail, Contacts, Calendars screen.

3 Scroll down the screen and then tap **Default Account**.

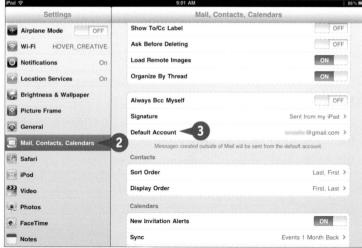

The Default Account Screen appears.

The current default account is shown with a check mark next to it.

④ Tap the account that you want to use as the default.

● A check mark appears next to the email account you tapped.

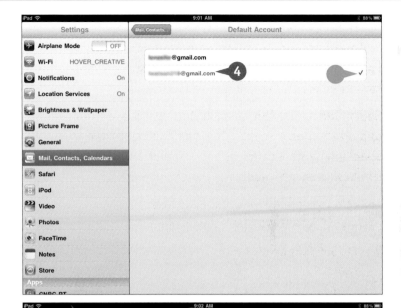

⑤ Tap the **Mail, Contacts, Calendars** button.

Your iPad returns to the Mail, Contacts, Calendars screen.

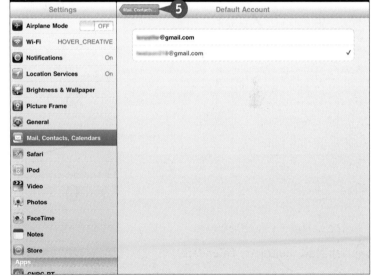

How does the Mail app choose the default email account once you have more than one?
The Mail app specifies the first email account that you created on the iPad as the default email account. When you create an email message from other iPad apps, such as Photos or Safari, or by tapping the email address in Contacts, it is sent using the default email account.

Switch to Another Email Account

The average person can have at least three email accounts. One main account and two backup accounts, usually one for school, if the person is a student, and one for work. When you tap the Mail app on the Home screen, you are taken to the last screen that was shown in your previous Mail session. You can also switch from the current account to view the contents of the Inbox for your other iPad mail accounts with just a few taps of your finger.

The ability to switch between accounts enables you to monitor the activities of multiple accounts and stay up to date.

Switch to Another Email Account

1 Tap **Mail** on the Home screen.

Note: The Mail app opens to whatever screen you viewed last, so if you viewed the Inbox last, the app displays the contents of the Inbox.

2 Tap the **Mail Address** button that appears in the top left corner of the screen.

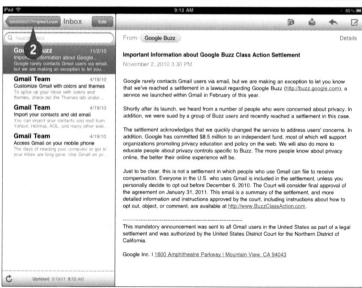

3 Tap the mailbox you want to view.

● You can tap **All Inboxes** to view a list of emails from all of your iPad email accounts.

● Tap a mailbox in the Accounts section to view an email account's folders such as Drafts, Sent Mail, Starred, and synced folders.

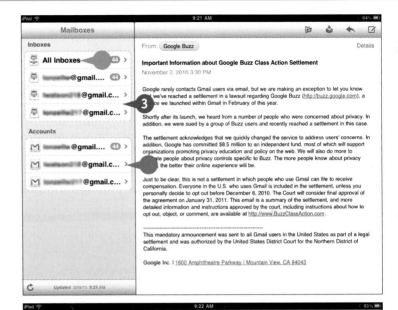

The mail for the new account appears.

4 Repeat steps **2** and **3** to view the contents of another account's Inbox.

If I change the settings for one of my email accounts on my iPad, will it change the settings on my computer when I sync?
No. Your email account settings can be synced only from your computer to your iPad, not the other way around. This enables you to customize your email settings for an email account on your iPad without changing email account settings on your computer.

Disable an Email Account

Over time, some of the email accounts that you have set up on your iPad may become irrelevant, or you may find that you just do not need to check them as often. There is a good reason for disabling accounts for which you do not have a pressing need. The Mail app on the iPad continuously checks for new emails for the accounts you have created. This repeated checking for email can more or less drain your battery power. You can temporarily disable an email address to conserve more of your battery power. Disabling an email account does not remove the account information from your iPad.

Disable an Email Account

1 Tap **Settings** on the Home screen.

The Settings screen appears.

2 Tap **Mail, Contacts, Calendars**.

The Mail, Contacts, Calendars screen appears.

3 Tap the account you want to disable.

The account's settings appear.

④ Tap **Mail** to the **Off** position.

⑤ Tap **Calendar** to the **Off** position.

Note: When you attempt to turn **Calendars** to **Off** for a Gmail account, for example, you receive an alert informing you that "All Gmail Calendars will be removed from your iPad."

⑥ Tap **Delete** in the Turn Off Calendars warning box.

⑦ Tap **Notes** to the **Off** position.

⑧ Tap **Done**.

The email account is disabled.

TIP

Are there other ways I can save battery power other than disabling an email account?

There are many, but in regard to email, you can do a few things in particular. Accounts such as Microsoft Exchange, MobileMe, and Yahoo! are referred to as *push* accounts. This means that when new messages are available, they are pushed/delivered to your iPad. This can eat your battery power, so consider turning off Push in the Mail settings. You can also check fewer email accounts by deleting an account or reduce the Fetch interval frequency. Consider ceasing all wireless activities by putting your iPad into Airplane mode.

Use a Different Server Port

Most of the time, sending email on your iPad is performed without any issues. On rare occasions, you may set up a new account and run into problems sending emails. As you attempt to send an email, it could seem that your iPad is slowly turning it wheels, and then you receive a message that informs you that a port has timed out.

If you are experiencing problems sending email from your POP account, try changing the outgoing server port to solve the issue. You can contact your ISP prior to specifying another port to make sure it is not blocking the port to which you want to switch. If you are unfamiliar with this process, you can also ask your ISP for guidance in acquiring a new port number.

Use a Different Server Port

1 Tap **Settings** on the Home screen.

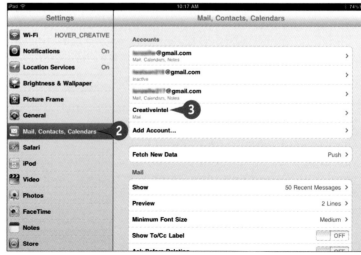

The Settings screen appears.

2 Tap **Mail, Contacts, Calendars**.

The Mail, Contacts, Calendars screen appears.

3 Tap the POP account you want to edit.

The account's settings appear.

④ Scroll down to the bottom of the screen and then tap **Advanced**.

The Advanced screen appears.

⑤ Tap **Server Port** in the Incoming Settings section.

The on-screen keyboard appears.

⑥ Type the port number.

What if I still experience outgoing email problems?
Check to see if all your settings are accurate. If you are still experiencing problems, call your ISP to verify if your account is set up correctly in the Mail app. Your ISP also can alert you to any policy conflicts that may be preventing you from sending email from a specific account.

Configure Authentication for Outgoing Mail

Your iPad does not have a built-in spam filter. If you are using an account such as Gmail, you get spam filtering on the server and junk mail goes straight to the Spam folder. Fortunately, some ISPs have security measures in place.

Authentication is a safety measure used to confirm that you are indeed the sender of the email and not a spammer. If your ISP requires authentication for outgoing mail, you can set up your email account to provide the appropriate credentials. The specification of a username and password is a common type of authentication.

Configure Authentication for Outgoing Mail

1 Tap **Settings** on the Home screen.

The Settings screen appears.

2 Tap **Mail, Contacts, Calendars**.

The Mail, Contacts, Calendars screen appears.

3 Tap the POP account you want to edit.

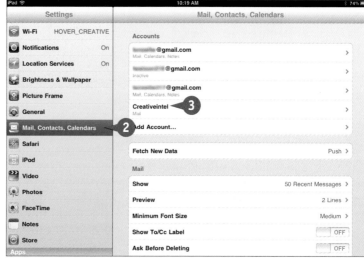

82

The account's settings appear.

④ Scroll down and tap **SMTP**.

The SMTP screen appears.

⑤ Tap in the **Primary Server** field.

⑥ Tap **Authentication** in the Outgoing Mail Server section.

The Authentication screen appears.

⑦ Tap an authentication option.

The authentication option has now been changed for the email account.

Note: Your ISP may require a specific authentication option.

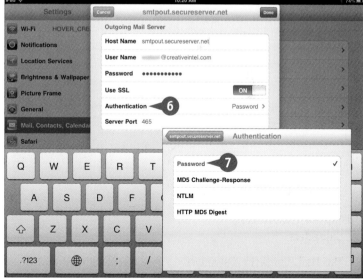

TIP

How many ISPs require authentication?
Most ISPs now require SMTP (Simple Mail Transfer Protocol) authentication for outgoing mail because of problems with junk email. You can check with your ISP to see if this applies to your service.

Automatically Check for New Emails

By default, the Mail app manually checks for new email messages whenever you tell it to. This is done by simply checking the Inbox for an account or by tapping the **Refresh** button (⟳) on the left side of the menu bar. Occasionally, you may want your iPad to automatically check for emails. This feature can come in handy if you are preoccupied and waiting for an important email. If the sounds on your iPad have not been muted, you hear a chime when you have received an email.

While you are considering this option, keep in mind that this incessant checking for emails does take a toll on your battery power.

Automatically Check for New Emails

1 Tap **Settings** on the Home screen.

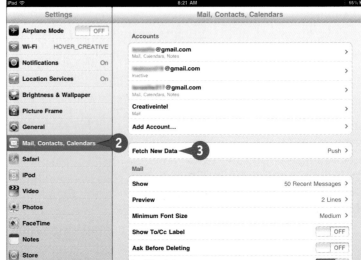

The Settings screen appears.

2 Tap **Mail, Contacts, Calendars**.

The Mail, Contacts, Calendars screen appears.

3 Tap **Fetch New Data**.

The Fetch Data screen appears.

④ Tap the interval you want to use in the Fetch section.

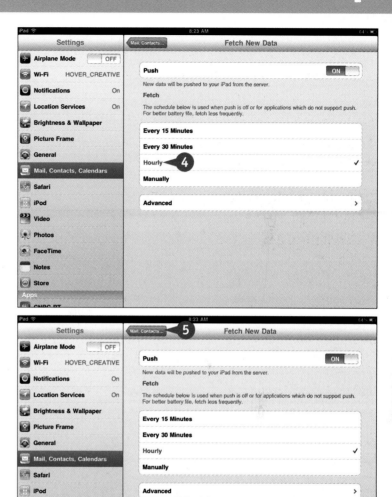

⑤ Tap the **Mail, Contacts, Calendar** button to return to the previous screen.

⑥ Repeat steps **1** to **4** to return to manually checking for new emails.

Should I keep my iPad set to automatically check mail?

To conserve battery power, you should consider returning your iPad to manually checking for new messages. You could also configure your iPad to check for new emails less frequently by choosing **Every 30 minutes** or **Hourly**. If you find the use of battery life miniscule, by all means, continue to have your iPad check for messages at regular intervals. If you have multiple accounts, you set different fetch rules for each account on the Advanced screen.

Email a Link to a Web Page

The iPad makes it easy for you to share links to interesting websites that you may come across with family and friends. You can send a link via email with just a few taps.

Some websites include an option to email a link, but in the absence of such an option, the iPad always gives you the Mail Link to this Page option. No more copying and pasting a link into the body of an email. The ability to email links makes it easy for you to share the good stuff from your findings on the web.

Email a Link to a Web Page

1 Tap **Safari** on the Home screen.

The Safari app opens.

2 Tap the **URL** field and then type the web address for the website you want to email.

● You can also perform a search with the search field to navigate to the site you want to email.

3 Tap **Go**.

Safari takes you to the website.

Note: If you performed a search, the search results appear, from which you can tap to open the desired web page.

④ Tap the **Share** button (⬆) on the menu bar.

A dialog with several options opens.

⑤ Tap **Mail Link to this Page**.

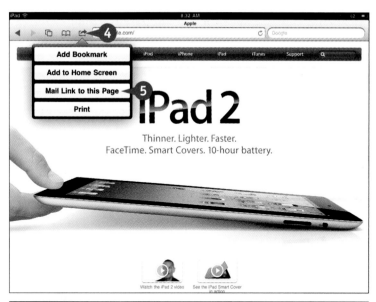

A new email message opens.

⑥ Type an email address or choose a recipient from your Contacts list.

Note: An email address must be listed for the contact if you choose someone from your Contacts list as a recipient.

Note: You can edit the message if you need to.

⑦ Tap **Send**.

The message is sent to the recipient.

TIP

Are there other ways to email website links?
Yes. But some of them are not as streamlined as choosing the Mail Link to this Page option found in Safari. You can copy the URL of the web page and then open the Mail app and paste the URL into a new message. Some websites are equipped with an option similar to the Mail Link to this Page option that can be found somewhere on the web page. The mail option in Safari is a quick solution.

Set Message Font Size

I f you are having a hard time reading your emails due to a small font size, your iPad makes it easy for you to change the font size for emails. iPad also enables you to automate the process so that you do not have to change the font size for each individual email that you receive.

You can set a minimum font size for emails, making them easier for you to read. If an email uses a larger font size than you specify, the font remains as is. If the font is smaller, your iPad scales up the font size accordingly.

Set Message Font Size

1 Tap **Settings** on the Home screen.

The Settings screen appears.

2 Tap **Mail, Contacts, Calendars**.

The Mail, Contacts, Calendars screen appears.

3 Tap **Minimum Font Size**.

The Minimum Font Size screen appears.

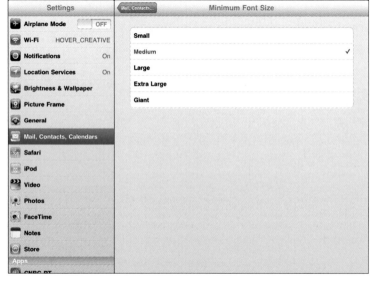

④ Tap the minimum font size you want.

⑤ Tap the **Mail, Contacts, Calendars** button to return to the previous menu.

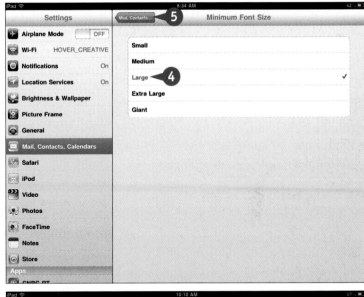

The Mail app now uses the minimum font size you have specified when displaying messages.

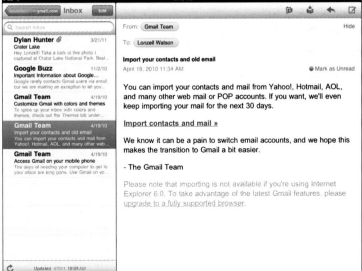

What can I do if I have trouble seeing an app on my iPad?
The iPad is equipped with a Zoom feature, which allows you to zoom into any app. You can use the Zoom feature to magnify the entire screen up to five times the normal size for increased readability. This feature works on the Home, Unlock, and Spotlight screens. You can also magnify apps that you purchase from the App Store. By default, the Zoom feature is disabled. To enable it, you must configure the triple-click function in the Settings under Accessibility.

Create a Custom iPad Signature

Do you have a favorite quote or slogan? The Mail app enables you to customize your own email signature, the same as you would in the mail program on your Mac or Windows computer. Creating a custom signature enables you to add your own personal touch to the bottom of outgoing email messages in the form of a block of text displaying your contact information or a short quote. Do not be afraid to be original or to sell yourself by listing your job title, degrees and certificates earned, or awards won. The proper signature could add just the right professional touch to your email correspondence.

Create a Custom iPad Signature

1 Tap **Settings** on the Home screen.

The Settings screen appears.

2 Tap **Mail, Contacts, Calendars**.

The Mail, Contacts, Calendars screen appears.

③ Tap **Signature**.

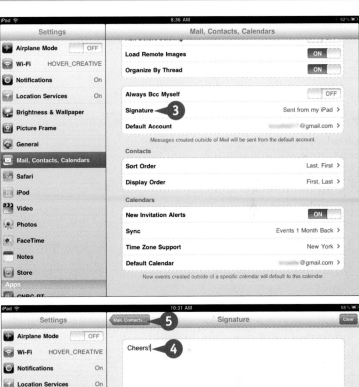

The Signature screen appears along with the on-screen keyboard.

Note: If you need to type a whole word or phrase in all caps, you do not need to keep tapping the Shift key. Double-tap the Shift key on the keyboard to type consecutive letters in all caps. Tap it once again to disable caps when you are finished.

④ Type the signature that you want to use.

Note: An email signature can be as short as one word, such as "Cheers," to a complete quote. Short is best.

⑤ Tap **Mail, Contacts, Calendars**.

The Mail app saves your signature and uses it for all outgoing email messages.

TIP

Can I return to the original signature?
The Mail app does not provide a way to cancel your edit and return to the original signature itself, but you can always write in "Sent from my iPad" yourself. Consider adding a personal line of your own and then place "Sent from my iPad" underneath it so the recipient knows the message originated from your iPad.

Disable Remote Message Images

You can disable images in the emails that you receive for faster load times and, more importantly, to help protect your privacy. If an image sent to you in an email is not attached to the actual email but kept on a remote server, your email will have to connect to the server to download the image. In the case of junk mail, this can open you up to "web bugs." Essentially, when you download the image from a remote server, the sender can find out personal information about you that could be used for marketing purposes. By disabling remote message images, you can help protect your personal information.

Disable Remote Message Images

1 Tap **Settings** on the Home screen.

The Settings screen appears.

2 Tap **Mail, Contacts, Calendars**.

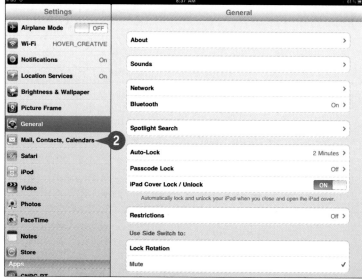

The Mail, Contacts, Calendars screen appears.

③ Scroll down and tap the **Load Remote Images** switch to the **Off** position.

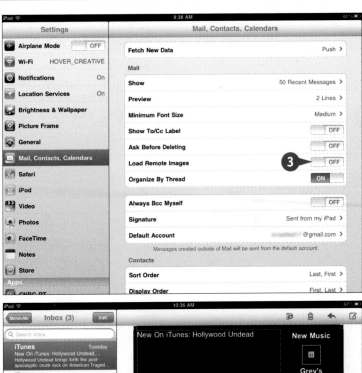

The setting is saved, and your iPad no longer displays remote images in your emails.

④ Press the Home button to return to the Home screen.

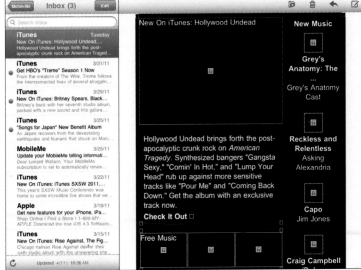

What exactly is a web bug?
A *web bug* is a reference embedded into HTML-formatted emails to images that reside on a remote server. When you open the email and image, Mail downloads the image by using an address for the remote server. In doing this, marketers can learn information about you and track your surfing habits across the Internet. Websites can also contain web bugs.

CHAPTER 5

Sync the iPad

Your iPad is a fully capable, stand-alone device, but you can also share much of the content on your computer with your iPad. Content found on your computer, such as apps downloaded from the App Store, iTunes music, movies, TV shows, calendar events, and contacts, are just some of the things you can share with your iPad. In this chapter, you learn how to connect your iPad to your computer and sync your fun — as well as productive — content with your iPad by using iTunes.

Connect Your iPad to a Computer

onnecting your iPad to your computer is one of the most basic ways of sharing content. If you do not have a MobileMe account, this is the primary way that you will keep all your contacts, calendars, and notes in sync between both devices. Once you have connected your iPad to your Mac or PC, you can begin syncing/sharing content between your computer and your iPad. Share photos taken on your iPad with your computer so that you can edit them in a photo-editing program. Share songs you have downloaded from iTunes on your Mac or PC with your iPad and vice versa.

Connect Your iPad to a Computer

1 Turn on your computer.

2 Place the USB end of the USB to Dock connector into a USB port on your computer.

3 Turn on your iPad.

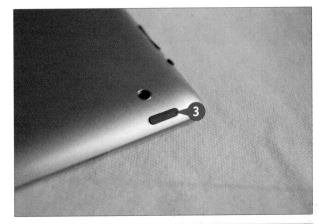

4 Attach the USB to Dock connector to your iPad.

Your iPad charges as it is connected to your computer.

TIPS

Can I connect my iPad to the computer by using iPad accessories?

Yes. If you want to use the iPad dock or iPad keyboard dock while using your iPad, you can run the USB to Dock cable to your computer from either of these docks rather than directly from the iPad. Make sure that you purchase the proper iPad dock for your specific iPad model.

My iPad does not charge when connected to my computer. Why?

You should make sure that all cables are connected securely; if that does not work, you should try using another USB port. If you have your iPad connected to the USB port located on your keyboard, try moving the iPad to a USB port located on the actual computer. The USB port located on the keyboard may not transfer enough power to charge the iPad. Even with a direct connection, some older Macs and many Windows computers do not provide enough power to charge the iPad. The USB specification calls for a minimum of 5 watts to charge the iPad.

Set Up a New iPad with iTunes

When you first set up your new iPad with iTunes, you can choose to set it up from scratch or restore from a previous backup. The second option can save you a lot of time if you have an extensive app collection and settings for a previous device such as your iPhone, first-generation iPad, or iPod touch.

You can determine if music, photos, and apps are synced automatically when you connect your iPad and launch iTunes. If you prefer to sync manually, you can prevent your iPad from syncing automatically.

Follow these steps after you have launched iTunes, registered your iPad, and read the iPad Software License Agreement.

Set Up a New

1 Click **iPad** in the Devices list.

2 Select the **Set up as a new iPad** radio button (○ changes to ●).

3 Click **Continue**.

4 Type a name for your iPad.

5 Leave the three check boxes deselected.

Note: This example does not select any of the check boxes so that manually syncing content can be shown later in the chapter.

6 Click **Done**.

The Info screen appears.

④ Click the **Sync iCal Calendars** check box (☐ changes to ☑).

Note: In Windows, click **Sync calendars with** (☐ changes to ☑) and then choose the program you want to use.

⑤ Click the **All calendars** radio button (◯ changes to ◉) to sync all calendars.

● You can click the **Do not sync events older than 30 days** check box (☐ changes to ☑) to control how far back the calendar sync goes. You can also type another value in the Days field.

⑥ Click **Apply**.

The selected calendars are synced to your iPad.

TIP

I have multiple calendars. How do I select just one of them?
If you have multiple calendars, you can sync only the calendars you want by clicking the **Selected calendars** radio button (◯ changes to ◉) in the Calendars field. After you make this selection, the field listing your other calendars is no longer grayed out. Click the check boxes (☐ changes to ☑) next to the calendars in the list that you want to sync.

☑ **Sync iCal Calendars**

◯ All calendars
◉ Selected calendars
☐ Home
☑ Work

Sync Your Email Account

iTunes makes it easy for you to sync email accounts, including your MobileMe account, Outlook, and Windows Mail, to your iPad. You can sync your mail account settings in the Mail Accounts sections located under the Info tab. You can choose to synchronize all of your email accounts or just individual accounts. Once you sync your accounts to your iPad, you can configure those accounts by tapping **Settings** and accessing the Mail, Contacts, Calendars option. Syncing your Mac or PC email accounts with your iPad is a great way to stay up to date with email messages when you are on the move.

Sync Your Email Account

① Connect your iPad to your computer.

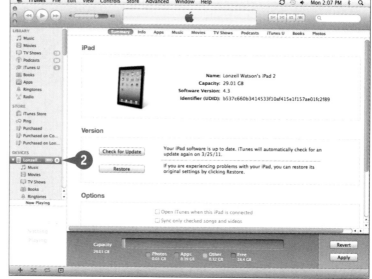

iTunes launches automatically on your computer. Your iPad appears in the Devices list.

② Click your iPad in the Devices list.

3 Click the **Info** tab.

The Info screen appears.

4 Click the **Sync Mail Accounts** check box (☐ changes to ☑).

Note: In Windows, click the **Sync selected mail accounts from** check box (☐ changes to ☑), choose your email program from the drop-down list, and then click the appropriate check box (☐ changes to ☑) for each account.

5 Select the mail accounts you want to sync to your iPad (☐ changes to ☑).

6 Click **Apply**.

Note: Click **Allow** if you receive a message asking if AppleMobileSync can be allowed access to your keychain.

iTunes syncs the email accounts you have specified to your iPad.

TIP

If I have an email account already set up on my Mac or PC and not on my iPad, can I sync to configure my iPad with the new account?

Yes. An easy way to configure your iPad with an existing email account on your Mac or PC is to instruct iTunes to share the information with your iPad through syncing. During the sync, iTunes shares all the account information with your iPad and establishes the new account.

Sync Your Bookmarks

Over time, you can accumulate a large number of bookmarks for websites on your computer and your iPad. It can be frustrating if you are on your iPad and need a bookmark you created on your computer. There is a convenient way for you to access those bookmarks. iTunes enables you to access those bookmarks by syncing them to your iPad.

When you sync your bookmarks, you are sharing the bookmarks that you have created within Safari or Internet Explorer on your Mac or PC so you can easily access those websites from your iPad.

Sync Your Bookmarks

① Once you connect your iPad to your computer, turn on the computer.

iTunes launches automatically on your computer. iPad appears in the Devices list.

② Click your iPad in the Devices list.

③ Click the **Info** tab.

The Info screen appears.

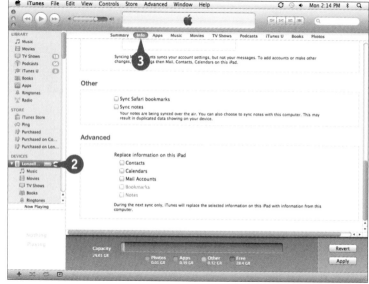

4 Scroll down to the Web Browser section and then click the **Sync Safari bookmarks** check box (☐ changes to ☑).

Note: In Windows, click the **Sync bookmarks with** check box (☐ changes to ☑) and then select the web browser from the list.

5 Click **Apply**.

Your bookmarks begin to sync from your computer to your iPad.

Any tips on syncing bookmarks?
Yes. Over time, you can accumulate many bookmarks on your computer. Some of these bookmarks may be to websites no longer relevant to you and that you no longer visit. Before you sync those bookmarks to your iPad, go through the bookmarks on your computer and then delete the ones no longer relevant. This way, you share only the important sites.

Sync Music, Music Videos, and Movies

Your iPad is great for listening to music and watching music videos you may have downloaded from iTunes. The primary way for you to move a large amount of content from your computer to your iPad is to sync. If your iPad has the storage capacity to hold all the music and music videos that you have downloaded to your computer, you can sync your entire library to your iPad. If you have a vast music library that exceeds the capacity of your iPad, you can configure iTunes to sync only the playlists, artists, genres, and videos that you want to share with your iPad.

Sync Music, Music Videos, and Movies

Note: You should already have your iPad connected to your computer before following these steps.

① Click your iPad in the Devices list.

② Click the **Music** tab.

The Music screen appears.

③ Click the **Sync Music** check box (☐ changes to ☑).

Note: iTunes may ask you to confirm that you want to sync music.

④ Click the **Selected playlists, artists, albums, and genres** radio button (○ changes to ◉).

⑤ Select the playlists, artists, albums, or genres you want to sync by clicking the check box next to them (☐ changes to ☑).

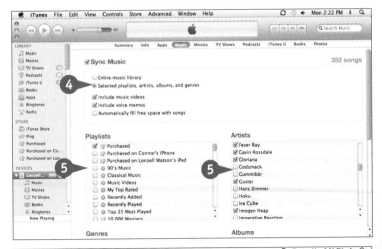

⑥ Deselect the **Include voice memos** check box (☑ changes to ☐) to exclude them from the sync.

⑦ Click **Apply**.

The playlists, artists, albums, and genres you have selected are synced to your iPad.

Can I transfer individual songs that I want to my iPad?

Yes. You can manage your music manually by connecting your iPad to your computer and then clicking **Music** in the Source list. You can drag the individual songs that you want from your music library and then drop them on top of your iPad in the Devices list to sync just those songs.

How do I sync my movies?

You can sync movies much in the same way that you synced music in the above task. Click the **Movies** tab in iTunes, and then click the **Sync Movies** check box to select it (☐ changes to ☑). You can choose individual movies to sync or automatically select all movies, most recently added movies, or unwatched movies.

Sync Podcasts

A long with downloading podcasts straight from your iPad, iTunes offers a solution for transferring podcasts downloaded to your Mac or PC. You can sync your favorite podcasts to your iPad so you can take them with you. Podcasts can range from just a few megabytes in size to tens of megabytes that can begin to eat into your iPad's storage space. If you have plenty of podcasts on your computer, then you need to manage what gets synced to your iPad. When you pick and choose only the podcasts that you want to sync to your iPad, you are using your storage capacity wisely.

Sync Podcasts

Note: You should already have your iPad connected to your computer before following these steps.

1 Click your iPad in the Devices list.

2 Click the **Podcasts** tab.

The Podcasts screen appears.

3 Click the **Sync Podcasts** check box (☐ changes to ☑).

4 Click the **Automatically include** menu to choose an option.

5 Click the **selected podcasts** menu to choose an option.

You can now choose individual podcasts contained within the available podcast series.

6 Click a podcast in the Podcasts field.

The podcast is highlighted, and the individual episodes appear to the right.

7 Select each individual episode that you want to sync to your iPad.

● If you want all the episodes that appear to the right of the podcast, you can just click the check box next to the podcast (☐ changes to ☑).

Note: Repeat steps **6** and **7** to choose new podcasts and individual episodes.

8 Click **Apply**.

iTunes syncs the iPad with the specified podcast episodes.

Can I designate a podcast as unplayed?
Yes. A podcast is designated as unplayed if you have not played at least part of it in iTunes or on your iPad. If you play a podcast episode on your iPad, that information is relayed to iTunes the next time that you sync. You can mark an episode as unplayed by clicking **Podcasts** in the iTunes library, right-clicking a particular podcast, and then choosing **Mark as Unplayed** from the menu.

Sync Audiobooks

If you have yet to discover the pleasures of audiobooks, audiobooks are like books on tape for your iPad, iPhone, and iPod. They play just like music tracks. You can sync audiobooks that you have downloaded to your computer to your iPad and audiobooks that you have "ripped" from CDs and categorized as audiobooks. Although audiobooks do not have a tab like Music, Podcasts, and TV Shows, you can access audiobooks in a variety of other ways. One of those other ways is that you can create a playlist that contains only audiobooks. You can also scroll down under the Books tab and you will find Audiobooks below eBooks. Syncing audiobooks is a great way to take your books with you while you travel.

Sync Audiobooks

Note: You should already have your iPad connected to your computer before following these steps.

1 Click your iPad in the Devices list.

2 Click the **Books** tab.

The Books screen appears.

3 Click the **Sync Books** check box (☐ changes to ☑).

④ Click the **Selected books** radio button (○ changes to ⦿).

The book selection below becomes accessible.

⑤ Click the check box next to all the books you want to sync (☐ changes to ☑).

⑥ Click **Apply**.

The audiobooks are synced to your iPad.

If I have more than one audiobook, can I choose which ones I want to sync?

Yes. The names of the authors also appear in the Artists field. You can click the check box (☐ changes to ☑) next to the name of the author in the Artists field to choose only the audiobooks that you want to sync to your iPad.

How do I sync my audiobooks if I have chosen to manually manage music and videos under the Summary tab?

If you have chosen the manual option under the Summary tab, the Playlists, Artists, and Genres options are not available under the Music tab. You must click the **Books** category in the iTunes library and then drag and drop the audiobooks that you want onto your iPad in the Devices list.

Sync TV Show Episodes

You can sync TV shows that you have downloaded to your computer to your iPad. If you have downloaded many TV episodes, such as if you have subscribed to an entire season of a program, you could quickly fill up your iPad's storage capacity. iTunes makes it easy for you to select only the shows that you want. You can choose to sync only a select few episodes to your iPad to conserve storage capacity. iTunes can also determine which episodes are unwatched so that you can sync only those shows you have not viewed. Use your storage space wisely.

Sync TV Show Episodes

Note: You should already have your iPad connected to your computer before following these steps.

1 Click your iPad in the Devices list.

2 Click the **TV Shows** tab.

The TV Shows screen appears.

3 Click the **Sync TV Shows** check box (☐ changes to ☑).

4 Click the **Automatically include** menu to choose an option.

Note: This example uses the default setting.

5 Click the **selected shows** menu to choose an option.

You can now choose individual TV shows contained within the available TV series.

6 Click a TV show in the Shows list.

The TV show is highlighted, and the individual episodes appear to the right.

7 Select each individual episode that you want to sync to your iPad.

● If you want all the episodes that appear to the right of the TV show, you can just select the check box next to the show (☐ changes to ☑).

Note: Repeat steps **6** and **7** to choose new TV shows and individual episodes.

8 Click **Apply**.

iTunes syncs the iPad with the specified TV show episodes.

TIP

Can I designate a TV episode as unplayed?
Yes. A TV episode is designated as unplayed if you have not played at least part of it in iTunes or on your iPad. If you play a TV episode on your iPad, that information is relayed to iTunes the next time that you sync. You can mark an episode as unplayed by clicking the **TV Shows** tab in the iTunes library, right-clicking a particular episode, and then choosing **Mark as Unwatched** from the menu.

Sync Photos on Your Computer with Your iPad

The iPad Camera Connection Kit is a great way to transfer photos from your camera to your iPad. You also have the ability to capture photos directly from your iPad 2. If you already have a collection of your favorite photos located on your computer, you can sync your favorite photos on your computer to your iPad. Syncing is a very convenient way to move large quantities of photos from your computer to your iPad. You can sync photos that you have touched up or edited in a photo-editing application to show off your finished works when you travel.

Sync Photos on Your Computer with Your iPad

Note: You should already have your iPad connected to your computer before following these steps.

1 Click your iPad in the Devices list.

2 Click the **Photos** tab.

The Photos screen appears.

3 Click the **Sync Photos from** check box (☐ changes to ☑).

4 Choose an option from the pop-up menu.

Note: This example uses the default setting, iPhoto. You can also specify a folder by selecting **Choose folder**. In Windows, you can choose **My Pictures** or **Pictures**.

Note: What you choose here dictates the remaining steps. Because this example uses iPhoto, the following steps are for iPhoto.

● When you select a location from which to sync photos, iTunes shows you the number of photos in that collection at the top right of the screen, and the projected capacity it would require at the bottom of the screen.

5 Click the **Selected albums and events, and automatically include** radio button (◯ changes to ◉).

● You can click the **Include videos** check box (☐ changes to ☑) if you have recorded video in your photo album that you want to include.

6 Click the check boxes (☐ changes to ☑) for the events you want to sync to your iPad.

7 Click **Apply**.

The photo album you have selected syncs to your iPad.

What file types are compatible with my iPad?

Your iPad is compatible with the usual TIFF and JPEG file formats along with PNG, BMP, and GIF files. If you have photos in a format incompatible with your iPad, you must convert them to a compatible format before you can successfully sync them to your iPad.

Save Photos from Emails

Occasionally, friends and family members may send you an email with an image attachment. Your iPad displays image attachments in the following formats: JPEG, GIF, and TIFF. You can view that photo directly in the body of the email that you received, and you can also download the image and save it on your iPad.

You can access the saved images within the Photos app or you could even set it as wallpaper by accessing Brightness & Wallpaper under Settings. Saving images from emails is a great way to archive important photos and can be performed in just a few taps.

Save Photos from Emails

1 Tap **Mail** on the Home screen.

Your default email account opens.

2 Open the email that contains the photo you want to download.

3 Tap the attachment.

The photo downloads and appears in the email message.

Note: If the image is in a format incompatible with your iPad, you can see the name of the file, but you cannot download it.

④ Tap the **Share** button ( ).

The options to Reply, Forward, Save Image, or Print Image appear.

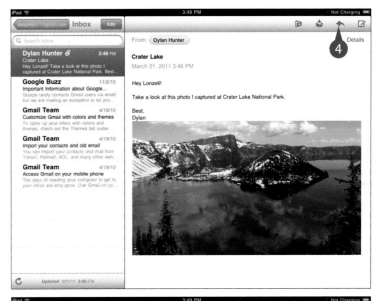

⑤ Tap **Save Image**.

The image is saved to a photo album and can be accessed with the Photos app.

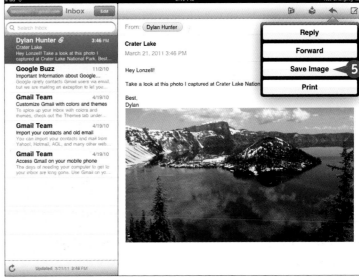

TIPS

Can I save video that I receive from an attachment?
Yes. But it needs to be an MP4 file. You can save video attachments sent to you by email much in the same way that you save photos. Just tap and hold the video attachment until the menu opens, giving you the option to save the video. Tap **Save Video** to save the video to your iPad.

Can I save an image on a website?
Yes. You can save an image that you find on a website to your iPad. After you open the web page that contains the image, tap and hold the image until you are given the option to save the image. Tap **Save Image** to save the website image to your iPad.

Import Photos from Your Camera

You have a number of options for importing your favorite photos to your iPad. You can sync photos on your computer to your iPad, you can collect them from email messages and websites, and you can also use the iPad Camera Connection Kit to download photos directly from your camera.

The iPad Camera Connection Kit enables you to connect your camera to your iPad by USB cable or by simply inserting a memory card into an attached SD card reader to import images. Whichever method you choose, you can connect the kit and begin importing your favorite photos in mere moments.

Import Photos from Your Camera

Connect with a USB Cable

1 Connect the USB to Dock adapter to the bottom of your iPad.

2 Attach one end of the USB cable into the adapter and the other end into the camera.

Note: The camera should be turned on and placed into Still Image mode if needed.

Connect an SD Card Connector

1 Connect the SD card reader to the 30-pin connector at the bottom of the iPad.

2 Insert the SD card from the camera into the slot.

Download Images

1 Click **Import All**.

The images begin to transfer.

TIP

Can I use an Apple USB keyboard with the iPad by attaching it with the USB connector in the camera connection kit?
No. But you can purchase an Apple Wireless Keyboard that uses Bluetooth technology with your iPad. As long as you are within range — around 30 feet of your iPad — you can move around freely with this keyboard. You may also want to consider the Apple iPad keyboard dock, which enables you to charge your iPad while using a full-sized keyboard.

CHAPTER 6

Explore iTunes, Photos, and Videos

Your iPad is packed with entertainment possibilities. You can use iTunes to preview, purchase, and download music, movies, TV shows, podcasts, and audiobooks. The Photos app offers a variety of ways to import and showcase your photos, including photo albums, slideshows, and using your iPad itself as a picture frame.

Discover What You Can Do with iTunes

Purchase Content

The iTunes Store has a wide variety of content to browse, including music, movies, TV shows, podcasts, audiobooks, games, and apps. Some content is free. Much of the content can be reviewed before you purchase, and you also have access to product descriptions and reviews from individuals who have previously purchased the content. Before you can make a purchase in the iTunes Store, you need to set up an iTunes account. Once you have set up an iTunes account, purchasing and downloading content is as simple as a few taps of your finger. You can scroll to the bottom of any page within iTunes and then tap **Sign In** to begin setting up an iTunes account.

Organize Content

Once you start downloading music, videos, and other content from iTunes, you can quickly amass a large library of content. iTunes on your computer is also a media management app that provides a number of ways to help you organize your content so that it is easy to find and use. You can organize apps with folders, remove individual videos, songs, and audiobooks from your iPad, create playlists, and burn discs.

Use Playlists to Manage Your Library

Creating playlists in iTunes is not only a great way to create a compilation of your favorite songs for playback, but playlists also provide you with further organization. You can use three types of playlists on your iPad: Standard Playlists, Genius Playlists, Genius Mixes, and Smart Playlists. You can make playlists from the music, podcasts, or audiobooks in your iTunes library. Understanding how to create a playlist can help you get the most from the iPod app on your iPad.

Sync Your Content

iTunes makes it easy for you to sync/share music, movies, TV shows, podcasts, audiobooks, email accounts, contacts, and calendars between multiple devices (iPhone, iPod touch, and iPad). You can also sync your MobileMe account or Outlook and Windows Mail to your iPad so you can check them while on the go and have easy access to current email messages.

Follow Artists and Music Fans

Ping is a social network for music available in iTunes. You can set up a free Ping profile to gain access to bios of artists and other Ping followers. You can follow your favorite artist and other Ping users to see what they have been up to and hear 30-second previews of what music they like and leave your own comments. See who is following whom and check out your favorite artist's or band's concert page to see where they are performing next. You can also automatically tweet your Ping activity and add people you follow on Twitter who also have a Ping profile.

Set Up an iTunes Account

You can also purchase music, movie, apps, and audiobooks in the iTunes Store and download hours of free educational content from iTunes U (University). To purchase content from iTunes, you first need to set up an iTunes account.

You will need an Apple ID to log in. If you have made purchases in the Apple Online Store, the App Store, or have a MobileMe account, you can sign into the iTunes Store using the same Apple ID. If you do not have an Apple ID, you must create one. You can create an Apple ID on your computer, iPhone, iPod touch, or your iPad.

Set Up an iTunes Account

1 Tap **Settings** on the Home screen.

The Settings screen appears.

2 Tap **Store**.

3 Tap **Sign In**.

A menu appears.

4 Tap **Create New Apple ID**.

5 Follow the prompts to create a new Apple ID.

You can now make purchases in the iTunes Store on your iPad.

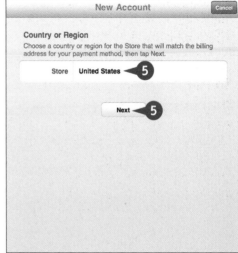

Buy and Download in iTunes

After you have set up your iTunes account, purchasing and downloading music, movies, TV shows, and other content are very easy tasks. Once you understand how to purchase and download content from iTunes, you can begin to populate your iPad with a wide variety of entertaining and educational content.

Take advantage of content previews. Just about every movie or song has a preview so that you can make an informed purchase. iTunes also has plenty of free content, so be sure to check out Free On iTunes under Featured music. The process for downloading free content is almost identical to paid content.

Buy and Download in iTunes

① Tap **iTunes** on the Home screen.

iTunes opens.

② Navigate to the content that you want to purchase.

③ Tap the price next to the content that you want.

The Price button changes to the Buy button.

Note: The Buy button is contextual, so if you are purchasing an album, it reads Buy Album. If you are buying a single, it reads Buy Single.

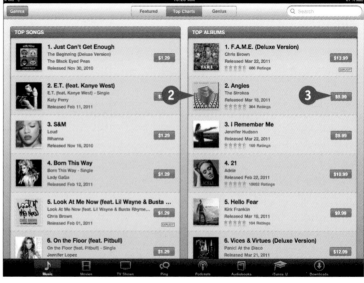

④ Tap the **Buy** button.

If you are not signed in or do not have an iTunes account, a Sign In screen appears.

⑤ Tap **Use Existing Apple ID** if you already have an iTunes account.

● If you do not have an iTunes account, tap **Create New Apple ID** to create an iTunes account.

The iTunes Password dialog opens.

⑥ Type your username.

⑦ Type your password.

⑧ Tap **OK**.

iTunes begins to download your purchase.

Note: You may be prompted to read new iTunes terms and conditions. If so, tap **OK**, read the terms and conditions, and then tap **Agree**. You will then have to attempt your purchase again.

Note: If this is your first time making a purchase on your new iPad, you will be prompted to edit your payment information as a security measure.

Can I transfer and play purchased content from iTunes on my other computers?
Yes. You can play content that you have purchased on iTunes on up to five authorized computers, either Mac or Windows or both. Authorization is used to protect the copyright of purchased content on iTunes. To authorize a computer, you must open iTunes on that computer, choose **Store**, and then choose **Authorize Computer** from the main menu bar. You will be required to type the password to your iTunes Store account. Devices such as an iPad, iPod, or iPhone do not count as a computer. You can deauthorize a computer by choosing **Store** and then **Deauthorize Computer** from the main menu bar.

Subscribe to Podcasts

Podcasts are downloadable radio- and TV-style shows. iTunes has a wide variety of audio and video podcasts, ranging from old-time radio classics to sports, science, and your favorite television shows. Be sure to check out iTunes U (University) by tapping on the iTunes U option at the bottom of the screen. iTunes U is a growing library of educational content where you can find lectures, films, labs, language lessons, audiobooks, and tours. As of this publication, all of the iTunes U content is free.

You can use iTunes to download podcasts straight to your iPad. Most podcasts are free, and you do not need an iTunes account to play or download podcasts.

Subscribe to Podcasts

① Tap **iTunes** on the Home screen.

iTunes opens.

② Tap **Podcasts** on the iTunes menu bar at the bottom.

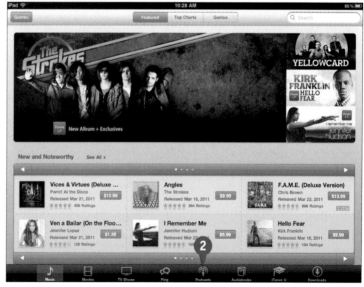

The Podcasts categories appear.

3 Navigate to a podcast that you want to download and then tap the podcast.

The podcast description appears, along with a list of the individual episodes.

Note: If you tap on a banner for a genre of podcasts, you are taken to a screen that displays all the available podcasts.

4 Tap the **Free** button for the episode that you want to download.

The Free button turns into the Get Episode button.

5 Tap **Get Episode**.

iTunes begins downloading the episode.

6 Repeat steps **3** and **4** to download more episodes.

Note: You can now close iTunes and then open the iPod app on your iPad to begin listening to your podcasts.

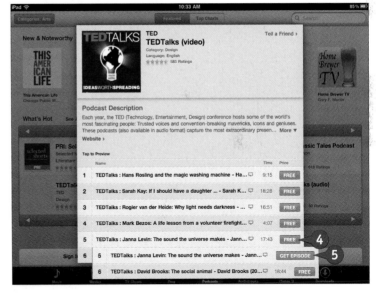

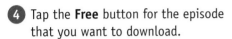

Can I subscribe to podcasts on my iPad?
No. But you can subscribe to a podcast within iTunes on your computer and then sync the new episodes to your iPad, iPhone, and iPod touch. Subscribing to your favorite podcast is a great way to have new episodes automatically download to your computer as they become available. You can also automatically update your podcast subscriptions from your computer.

What if I am unable to subscribe to a podcast?
If a podcast does not begin to download after you tap the **Get Episode** button, the website that hosts the podcast may be experiencing difficulties, so you might want to try again later. Another thing to consider is that some podcasts may use files incompatible with iTunes and iPad. It is rare, but if you suspect this, you should contact the producer of the podcast to receive more information.

Rate Content in the iTunes Store

iTunes uses a five-star rating system to rate all content. Just about all of the content on iTunes features reviews that you can read to see how others like the product. You can easily write reviews of your own to make your feelings known about the content you have purchased.

iTunes gives you the option of providing just a star rating for a product, but the more helpful information you can provide, the better. Rating content you have purchased on iTunes helps others to make educated decisions about their purchases on iTunes. You have to be logged into iTunes to rate content.

Rate Content in the iTunes Store

1 Tap **iTunes** on the Home screen.

iTunes opens.

2 Navigate to the content that you want to rate and then tap it.

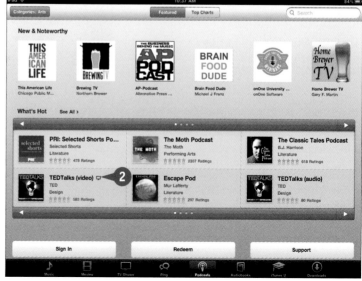

The content description page appears.

3 Scroll down toward the bottom of the content description page and then tap **Write a Review**.

iTunes takes you to the Write a Review page.

Note: If you are not logged in, iTunes prompts you to type your iTunes password. Log in to your account and then tap **OK**.

4 Tap the number of stars you give the content.

5 Type the title of your review.

6 Type your nickname.

7 Type your review.

8 Tap **Submit**.

The review is uploaded to iTunes.

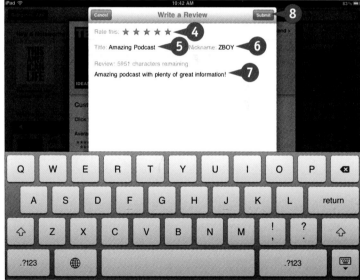

TIP

Can I rate content that I have not purchased on iTunes?

Yes. But unless you have experience with the product you are reviewing, you probably should not do this. Many individuals use the ratings and feedback you supply to make purchasing choices on iTunes, so you should provide the most accurate and sincere review possible.

Configure iPad Audio Settings

The iPod app on your iPad is where you can listen to your music, podcasts, and audiobooks. You can improve the sound quality of the audio tracks you listen to by changing the EQ settings. The EQ settings help to accentuate music from a wide range of genres including Rock, Hip Hop, Jazz, Piano, and Vocal Latin. You even have choices that can help improve podcasts and audiobooks with the Spoken Word and Vocal Booster options.

EQ settings immediately change the sound quality the moment you apply them. Some settings are more noticeable than others. Using the iPod EQ preferences enables you to customize your audio experiences on the iPad.

Configure iPad Audio Settings

1 Tap **Settings** on the Home screen.

The Settings screen appears.

2 Tap **iPod**.

The iPod settings appear.

3 Tap **Sound Check** to the **On** position to have iTunes play songs at the same level.

4 Tap **EQ**.

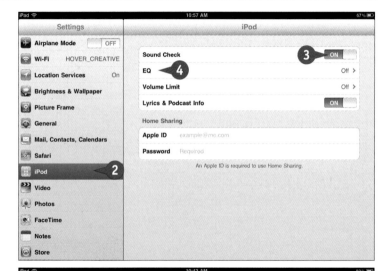

The EQ options appear.

Note: The EQ options are audio presets that you can choose to customize audio playback on your iPad.

5 Tap an EQ option to select it.

● A check mark appears next to the option you have chosen.

6 Tap **iPod**.

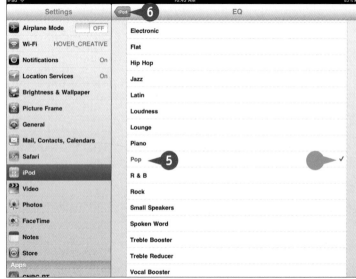

iPad returns to the iPod settings screen.

● You can leave Lyrics & Podcast Info set to On to display lyrics and podcast information.

7 Tap **Volume Limit** to set a maximum volume at which audio can be played back on your iPad.

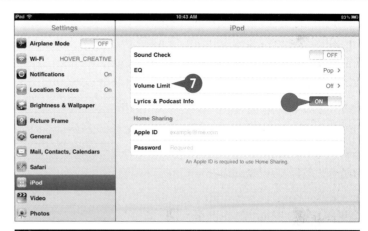

The Volume Limit slider appears.

8 Drag the slider to the desired level.

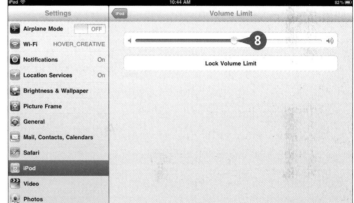

Is there any way that I can keep the volume limit from being changed once I set it?

Yes. You can set the volume limit by dragging the slider and then create a passcode that must be typed to change it. It is important that you remember the passcode. Follow these steps:

1 Tap **Lock Volume Limit** in the Volume Limit options.

2 Type a four-digit passcode.

3 Type the four-digit passcode again.

The volume limit is locked.

4 Tap **Unlock Volume Limit** and then retype the passcode to unlock the volume limit.

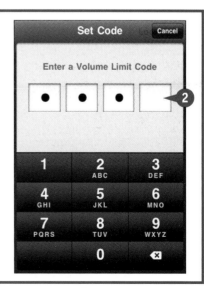

Browse and Play Content in the iPod App

The iPod app on your iPad was designed to make it easy for you to browse your music collection, podcasts, and audiobooks on your iPad. You can browse your content library by tapping categories including: Music, Podcasts, Audio books, and playlists. View your content in even more ways by choosing to view Songs, Artists, Albums, Genres, and Composers at the bottom of the screen.

You can use the built-in mono speaker in your iPad to play back content or use a set of headphones, a headset or external speakers for stereo sound. The ability to browse your iPod content library is the first step toward getting the most from the iPod app.

Browse and Play Content in the iPod App

1 Tap **iPod** on the Home screen.

The iPod app opens.

2 Tap the category for the content that you want to browse in the iPod library.

The contents for the category appear on the right-hand side of the screen.

Note: This example uses the Music category.

Note: Use your finger to scroll up and down the results in the list.

Note: For the Music and Purchased categories, you can sort content by Songs, Artists, Albums, Genres, and Composers.

The individual episodes appear on the left of the screen, and the artwork for the TV show appears on the right.

Note: If you tapped a movie under the Movies category, a movie description appears, supplying you with information about the downloaded file.

④ Tap the episode that you want to play.

The episode begins playing.

● You can also tap the **Play** button (▶) to begin playing all the episodes back to back.

Note: Consider watching videos in landscape orientation for the biggest picture.

⑤ Tap the screen to reveal the playback controls.

Note: You can watch movies on your iPad on a television screen. Use the Apple Component AV cable, Composite AV cable, Apple iPad Dock Connector to VGA Adapter, and other compatible connectors to connect your iPad to a TV or projector. Be sure that you make the proper adjustments for the TV OUT settings by going to Settings under Video.

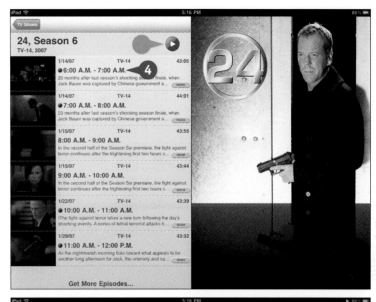

TIP

Can I transfer rented movies I purchase on my computer in iTunes?
Yes. You can transfer the rented movie to a supported iPhone, iPod, or AppleTV. Once you sync the movie to the new device the movie is removed from the iTunes library on your computer. You can transfer the movie between supported devices as many times as you want during the rental period, but you can play the movie on only one device at a time. Once you start playing the movie, you have to finish it within 24 hours. After 24 hours rented movies vanish from your iPad.

Customize Video Settings

You can tweak many of the built-in apps of your iPad by tapping **Settings** on your main Home screen. You can customize the video settings on your iPad to determine if videos you play back in the Videos app start where you left off, or if they should start at the beginning.

The video settings are also equipped with a feature that accommodates the hearing impaired. You can choose to turn on closed captioning by tapping a switch. If you would like to play your videos out to a television set, configure your iPad to play out to a widescreen TV. The ability to customize the video options on your iPad gives you more viewing options.

Customize Video Settings

1 Tap **Settings** on the Home screen.

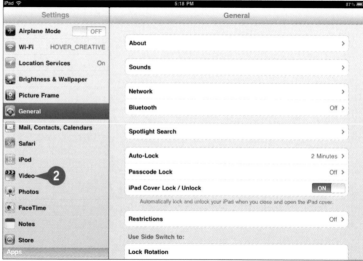

The Settings screen appears.

2 Tap **Video**.

The Video options appear.

③ Tap **Start Playing** to choose the starting point for videos after you have stopped them and want to replay them.

④ Tap **Closed Captioning** to the **On** position if you are hearing impaired.

Note: Some videos do not have closed captioning support. Check for the CC logo when purchasing.

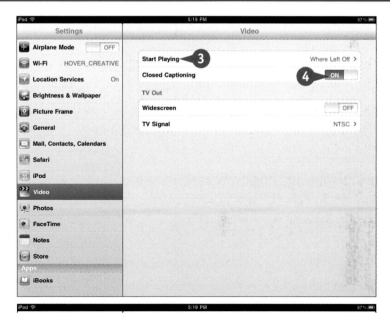

⑤ Tap **Widescreen** to the **On** position if you are playing widescreen video on your iPad out to a TV set.

⑥ Tap **TV Signal** to set whether the TV you are playing out to uses an NTSC or PAL signal.

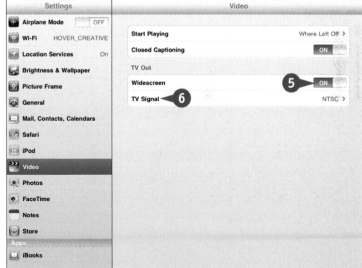

TIP

What are NTSC and PAL?

NTSC (National Television System Committee) and PAL (Phase Alternating Line) are the two major standard analog television encoding systems used in broadcast television. NTSC is used in North America and Japan, and PAL is used nearly everywhere else in the world.

Capture Photos with Your iPad 2

Along with the ability to sync photos from other devices and use the iPad Camera Connection Kit to acquire images, your iPad 2 is capable of capturing photos of its own. The Camera app can toggle between a still-image camera and a video camera. By default, your iPad 2 is in the still-image mode when you open Camera.

The big iPad screen makes it easy for you to compose a shot, but can become difficult to view in bright lighting conditions. You can review images as soon as you acquire them by tapping the Camera Roll thumbnail. Your iPad 2 is capable of housing literally thousands of photos.

Capture Photos with Your iPad 2

1 Tap **Camera** on the Home screen.

Camera opens.

2 Move the switch to still-image mode.

3 Compose the shot.

Note: An unrecognizable object off in the distance often does not make for great subject matter, so get close, if you can, so that your subject does not appear tiny.

4 Tap in the frame where you want Camera to focus.

Note: When you tap the screen to focus on the subject, Camera adjusts the overall exposure of the scene for that spot. If you tap in a bright area, the overall scene darkens so the main subject you specified has the proper exposure.

5 Press the **Shutter** button (⬚), and then lift your finger to capture the image.

Note: The image is not captured when you first touch the **Shutter** button (⬚), but after you release it.

146

The shutter sound effect is heard. A thumbnail of the image appears in the bottom left corner of the interface.

Note: The iPad's slow shutter makes it prone to producing blurry photos if you do not remain perfectly still during capture.

6 Tap the **Camera Roll** button.

The last image you captured appears on-screen.

● When you tap the screen, more options and controls appear at the top and bottom of the interface. You can tap **Camera Roll** in the upper left corner to view a thumbnail of all photos and videos captured at once.

7 Flick the screen to the left or right to review all photos you have captured.

● You can delete a photo by touching the screen to reveal more options and controls. Tap **Delete** ( ) to delete the current image on-screen.

8 Tap **Done** to return to Camera.

TIPS

How do I share my photos while in Camera View?

When you tap the screen, more options and controls appear at the top and bottom. Tap the **Share** ( ) button to email a photo, set a photo as wallpaper, print, or copy a photo.

Any more camera tips?

Yes. *Shutter lag* is the amount of time between pressing the Shutter Release button and the moment the picture is taken. Shutter lag can cause you to miss a shot of a moving subject. iPad 2 has a long shutter lag, so be mindful of your timing. The image is not captured when you first touch the Shutter button ( ), but after you release it. Use this to your advantage and have your finger on the shutter button in anticipation of the shot.

Shoot Video with Your iPad 2

Your iPad 2 places plenty of creative power at your fingertips, literally. The video capability of your iPad 2 is great for capturing those spontaneous yet fleeting moments that you want to remember.

With the release of the iPad 2, Apple has adopted one of the latest trends in digital still- and video-camera technology and utilized what is called a *backside-illuminates sensor*. This sensor improves the low-light performance of the iPad 2's camera by increasing light sensitivity and reducing noise (grain). You can review your footage immediately after recording in Camera Roll and easily share those videos with friends and family.

Shoot Video with Your iPad 2

① Tap **Camera** on the Home screen.

Camera opens.

② Move the switch to video mode.

③ Compose the shot.

Note: An unrecognizable object off in the distance often does not make for great subject matter, so get close, if you can, so that your subject does not appear tiny.

④ Tap the **Record** button (⦿).

The record button blinks (⦿ changes to ⦿). A timecode overlay appears in the upper right-hand corner as you record.

Note: Shaky video diminishes the quality of your video. Keep the iPad as still as possible as you record.

⑤ Tap the **Record** button (⦿) again to stop recording.

A thumbnail of the video appears in the bottom left corner of the interface.

6 Tap the **Camera Roll** button.

The last video you recorded appears on-screen for you to play.

● When you tap the screen, more controls appear at the top and bottom of the interface. You can tap **Camera Roll** in the upper left corner to view a thumbnail of all photos and videos at the same time.

7 Flick the screen to the left or right to review all of the videos and photos you have captured.

● You can delete a video by touching the screen to reveal more options and controls. Tap **Delete** (🗑) to delete the current video on-screen.

8 Tap **Done** to return to Camera.

TIPS

How do I share my videos while in Camera View?

When you tap the screen more options and controls appear at the top and bottom. Tap the **Share** (📤) button to email video, send to YouTube, or copy video.

Do you have more tips on shooting video?

Yes. Consider the position of the sun when shooting outdoors. Choose to shoot in an evenly lit area to lower the contrast. If you must shoot in direct sunlight, record the subject with the sun at your back and your subject facing your iPad.

Get Some FaceTime

iPad 2 makes it easy for you to stay in touch and see faraway friends and family with the introduction of video calls. The FaceTime app uses the front camera on your iPad so that other FaceTime users can see you and you can see them.

To video call someone, just find his name in your Contacts list, and then tap his email address. A message pops up on his Mac, iPad, iPhone 4, or iPod touch asking him if he wants to join you. When he accepts, you see his face on your iPad and he sees you. You must enable Wi-Fi on your iPad to use FaceTime.

Get Some FaceTime

Note: When you place a FaceTime call using a person's email address, the recipient must be signed into his Apple ID and have verified that email address for use with FaceTime.

1 Tap **FaceTime** on the Home screen.

FaceTime opens.

Note: If you have not enabled Wi-Fi on your iPad, FaceTime gives you a message that you need to turn on Wi-Fi. Tap **Yes** to enable or tap **Settings** to be taken to the settings.

2 Tap in the fields and type your Apple ID.

3 Tap **Sign In**.

Your FaceTime account has been created.

4 Tap in the **Address** field to change the email address, if needed.

5 Tap **Next**.

Your iPad Contacts list appears.

6 Tap a contact.

● You can tap **Groups** to view Contacts groups on your iPad.

● You can tap the plus sign (⊞) to add a new contact.

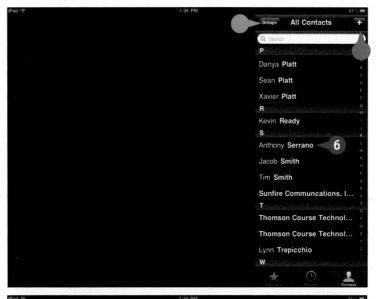

The contact's Info page opens.

7 Tap the email address of the contact to place the call.

A message pops up on the recipient's Mac, iPad, iPhone 4, or iPod touch asking him if he wants to join you. When he accepts, you see his face on your iPad and he sees you.

Note: You need the phone number or email address of the recipient to make a FaceTime call. If you are calling an iPhone 4, use the recipient's telephone number. If you are calling someone's iPad 2, use his email address.

● Tap **Add to Favorites** for easy access next time.

● Tap **Favorites** to access your favorites.

● Tap **Edit** to edit a contact's information.

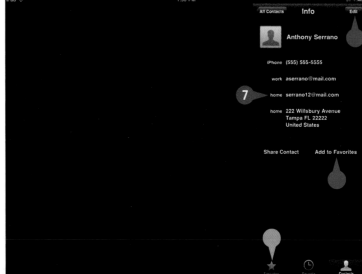

TIPS

Am I placing a FaceTime call over Wi-Fi or 3G networks?
As of this publication, Apple intended FaceTime to be used over Wi-Fi networks. This is not to say that no workarounds exist that allow you to use FaceTime over a 3G network. Perhaps iPad will support this feature at a later time. For the best performance of your iPad 2, use the features as Apple intended them to be used.

Can I place a FaceTime call within the Contacts app?
Yes. If you look at the bottom of a Contact's page you can see a tab named FaceTime. Tap the **FaceTime** tab to place your call to that contact.

View Photos on Your iPad

The Photos app enables you to view photos you have captured with your iPad 2, synced from your computer, or downloaded from your camera or a memory card. Photos can be managed as albums, events, faces, and places and are showcased in a high-quality display. Browsing photos has been optimized for the iPad's multi-touch screen so navigating Photos is as simple as a tap, flick, or pinch. Your iPad supports the JPEG, GIF, PNG, and TIFF image formats.

View Photos on Your iPad

① Tap **Photos** on the Home screen.

The Photos app opens.

② Tap the category of pictures you want to view.

③ Tap a collection to open it.

The photo collection opens.

Note: You can pinch your fingers shut on-screen to collapse the collection of photos.

④ Tap the photo that you want to view.

The photo opens. Controls appear at the top and bottom of the page. You can use the controls at the bottom of the screen to tap and open a new photo. The controls disappear after a few seconds or you can tap the screen once to make the controls disappear.

⑤ Tap a thumbnail to progress to the next photo.

Note: You can also turn the page with your finger to progress to the next picture.

Note: You can rotate the iPad to the proper orientation to view the photo.

Note: You can double-tap the photo to make it larger. Double-tap it again to have it return to its original size.

Note: You can perform a pinching motion with two fingers on-screen to enlarge the photograph and then pan the photo with one finger.

TIP

Can I upload photos to my MobileMe gallery?
Yes. You can even add photos to someone else's MobileMe account, if that person has set that option for his gallery. First, you must set up your MobileMe account on your iPad. Second, you need to publish a MobileMe gallery and configure it to allow photos from iPad. If you do not have a MobileMe account, you can set up one at www.me.com.

Send a Photo or Video by Email

Camera Roll and the Photos app make it very easy for you to share videos and photographs with others by emailing them to friends and family. You can access both photos and videos in the same list using Camera Roll. Your sharing options for photos are Email Photo, Use as Wallpaper, Print, and Copy Photo. You can Email Video, Send to YouTube, and Copy Video. All of these share options are accessible from both Camera Roll and the Photos app. In just a few taps, you can create a new email and place a photo in the body of the letter. Follow these directions from within Photos.

Send a Photo or Video by Email

① Tap the photo collection that contains the picture you want to mail.

The photo collection opens.

Note: To access a video you want to email, tap **Camera** on the Home screen, and then tap the **Camera Roll** button. To access videos, tap **Camera Roll** in the top left corner of the interface.

Note: Video clips are much larger files than photos. Choose short videos of just a few seconds to avoid any email file size issues.

② Tap the photo that you want to mail.

The photo opens.

3 Tap the **Share** button (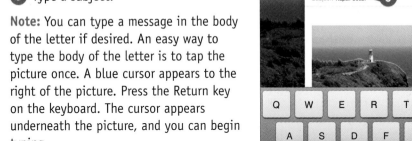).

A menu appears.

Note: You may need to first tap the screen to make 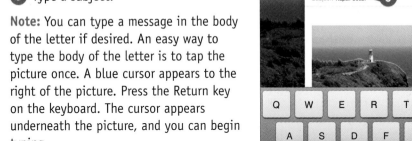 appear.

4 Tap **Email Photo**.

Note: You can also use this menu to add a photo to a contact or choose a photo as the wallpaper for your iPad.

A new email message is created, with the photo in the body of the letter.

5 Type the email address of the recipient.

6 Type a subject.

Note: You can type a message in the body of the letter if desired. An easy way to type the body of the letter is to tap the picture once. A blue cursor appears to the right of the picture. Press the Return key on the keyboard. The cursor appears underneath the picture, and you can begin typing.

7 Tap **Send**.

The message is sent to the recipient.

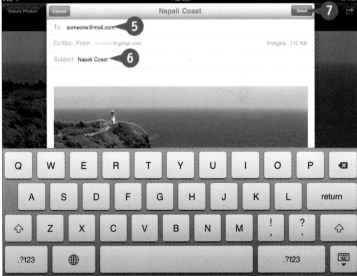

TIP

Does my iPad have screen saver capabilities?

Yes. The feature is called Picture Frame. When your iPad is locked, an icon of a sunflower () appears to the right of Slide to Unlock. When you tap that icon, iPad uses photos in your photo library as a slideshow while your iPad charges in the dock. You can adjust the settings of Picture Frame by tapping **Settings** on the Home screen. Under Settings, you can choose the type of transition you want between slides, the duration of the slides, a specific collection of photos for the slideshow, and more.

Create a Custom Slideshow

You can create a slideshow of any selected photo album or your entire iPad photo library using the Photos app. You can also create a slideshow of your photos and/or video within Camera Roll. Feel free to customize your slideshow by choosing your own music and transitions between photographs in the Photos app or in Camera Roll. Creating a customized slideshow is a quick way to preview a newly imported group of pictures on your iPad and then add your own personal touch.

Create a Custom Slideshow

1 Tap the photo collection that you want to view as a slideshow.

The photo collection opens.

2 Tap **Slideshow**.

The Slideshow options appear.

3 Tap **Transitions**.

The Transitions library appears.

4 Tap the transition you want to use.

The Transitions library closes.

Note: The default Dissolve transition is used in this example.

5 Tap **Play Music** to the **On** position.

6 Tap **Music**.

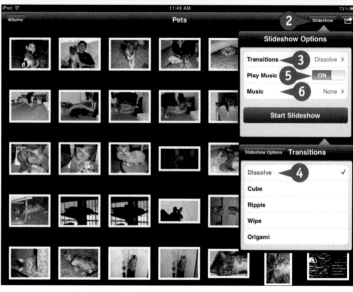

The music contained in your Music library appears.

7 Locate the music that you want to use and tap the track.

The Music library closes.

8 Tap **Start Slideshow**.

The slideshow begins to play full screen.

Note: Tap the screen once to stop the slideshow.

TIP

Can I set the duration for my slideshow?
Yes. You can change the duration for each slide, determine whether the slideshow repeats after it has finished playing, and set photos to shuffle. Follow these steps:

1 Tap **Settings** on the Home screen.

2 Tap **Photos**.

3 Customize the individual slideshow settings.

CHAPTER 7

Get the Most from YouTube and iBooks

Your iPad is an entertainment center packed with many options for you to experience the web and download materials for your own personal enjoyment. Your YouTube experience has been optimized for your viewing pleasure on the iPad. Your iPad is a highly capable e-reader with the ability to browse, purchase, and download books with the iBooks app.

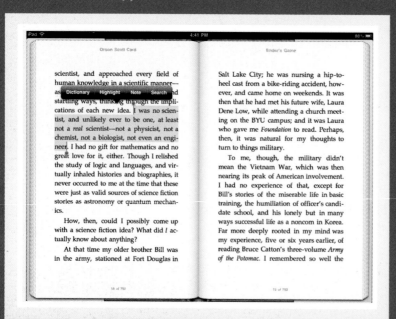

The iBooks Store opens.

3 Locate the book you want to purchase and download, and then tap the price.

The button changes to Buy Book.

Note: As you browse eBooks, you will find books available for free. Tap **Free** for free books to download. The button changes to Get Book after you tap it.

4 Tap the **Buy Book** button.

iBooks asks you to type your iBooks account password.

5 Type your iBooks account password.

6 Tap **OK**.

iBooks begins to download the eBook. The book cover appears on your bookshelf.

TIPS

Will I be charged twice if I attempt to download a book I have previously purchased?

Usually not. If you attempt to download a book that you have previously purchased, iBooks generally alerts you to this fact and asks if you would like to proceed with the download. If you are billed twice for the download, you can report a problem in the iBooks Store.

What are some other popular e-readers out there for me?

If you prefer a different e-reader, you can browse the App Store for other readers such as Kindle, Kobo, Nook, and Stanza.

Understand iBooks Navigation Controls

iBooks enhances your reading experience by offering reading aids such as the ability to increase font size, highlight text, take notes, and change background color. You can quickly search for words and phrases throughout a book, conduct a dictionary inquiry, as well as call upon other resources, such as the Google search engine or Wikipedia. iBooks provides the flexibility of instantly moving to specific locations within a book by tapping bookmarks and chapters in the table of contents.

Many of the iBooks features can be accessed at the top of book pages; other features are revealed in a pop-up menu when your press your finger to text, and then lift it.

Highlight Text and Take Notes

Once you find a page with a passage or quote that is a focal point, iBooks makes it easy for you to highlight the text and/or leave a note. Hold your finger to the passage, and then lift your finger to receive menu options to highlight or leave a note. Drag the blue handles to include the text that you want, and then tap **Highlight** or **Note**. A sticky is placed next to the note in the text. The default color for highlights is yellow, but you can tap the highlighted text again and choose another color. You can also remove highlights and notes by tapping the specified text a second time.

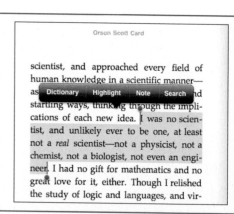

Perform a Dictionary Search

When you come across a word for which you do not know the meaning, iBooks enables you to conduct a quick dictionary inquiry. Press your finger to the text on-screen, position the handles around the word, and then tap **Dictionary** to receive definitions, phonetic pronunciations, usage of the word, and origin. Tap the screen again to make the dictionary information disappear.

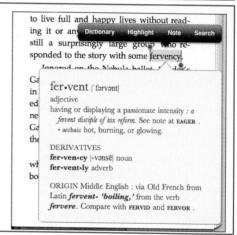

Bookmark Locations

Perhaps the most elementary of all the iBooks features is to place a bookmark at a location where you want to return in the future. When you close the iBooks app, it reopens to the same page where you stopped when you next launch iBooks. If you are reading material on your iPad for study purposes, you may be flipping back and forth between pages comparing information. In this scenario, where you stopped reading and closed iBooks may not be where you necessarily want to return next time you begin reading. You can bookmark where you want to pick up, or leave yourself a note regarding the page number.

Search for Words or Phrases

If you want to find each instance of a word or phrase in the book, you can use the search features in iBooks to locate it. Press your finger to the text on-screen, position the handles around the word that you want to search for, and then tap **Search** in the pop-up menu. A list of locations where that phrase was used appears, along with a brief excerpt. You can tap a location within the list to jump to that location. There are also options for you to Search Google or Search Wikipedia for the word or phrase. Clear the search field at the top and start a new search and tap the search icon (🔍) to start a new search at any point during your reading session

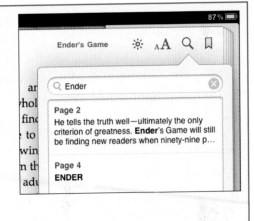

Jump to Locations

One of the benefits of eBooks is being able to jump from one location to another location within them, instantly, without thumbing through pages. iBooks provides a number of ways for you to achieve this. Touch a book page to reveal the iBooks controls. You can jump back to the table of contents at any point in the book by tapping the TOC icon (☰). The TOC page also lets you access your bookmarks so that you can return to those locations. The pagination of the book is close to what you get in paper format. A slider at the bottom of each page tells you what page you are on.

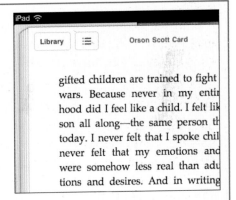

Adjust, Brightness, Font Size, and Background

Touching a book page toggles between revealing and hiding the iBooks controls located at the top and bottom of each page. The brightness of your iPad screen can be adjusted to accommodate the varying lighting conditions in which you read. Tap the brightness icon (☀) to adjust the screen. Tap the A icon (ᴀA) to enlarge the font size, choose a new font, and change the book background from white to sepia.

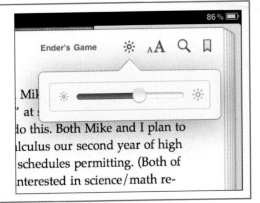

CHAPTER 8

Manage Contacts and Appointments

The iPad is equipped with the Contacts and Calendar apps that help you improve your efficiency when it comes to managing personal contacts and important appointments.

Create a New Contact

Your iPad is highly capable of helping you organize your important data. The Contacts app can help you manage the sensitive information you receive from friends, colleagues, and prospective business associates. Think of the Contacts app as your virtual Rolodex, filled with contact information such as names, physical addresses, emails, notes, and so on.

Contacts relieves you from worry of losing a business card. If you have a MobileMe account, all the information you gather in Contacts can be synced to your computer and updated automatically to your mobile devices. Understanding how to create a new contact helps you to manage your personal contacts.

Create a New Contact

1 Tap **Contacts** on the Home screen.

● You can tap the **FaceTime** tab at the bottom of the contact's page to place a video call.

● You can share a contact via email by tapping **Share contact**. A virtual business card for the contact is embedded in an email and sent to the recipient.

The Contacts app opens.

2 Tap the plus sign (+).

A new contact screen appears.

A blinking cursor appears in the box labeled First.

③ Tap each field and then type the information you have for the contact.

● If you want to note the phone line type, tap the field labeled **mobile** and then choose from the list that appears. You can make similar customizations to other fields including email and address information.

④ Tap **Done**.

Your iPad saves the information you have typed and takes you to the All Contacts screen.

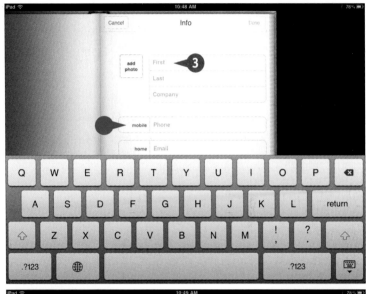

TIPS

Is it easy to delete a contact?
Yes. Tap the contact you want to delete, and then tap **Edit** in the bottom left corner of the page. Scroll to the bottom of the contact sheet and then tap **Delete Contact**. Tap **Delete Contact** again.

Can I search for a contact without opening the Contacts app?
Yes. The Spotlight Search feature of your iPad also searches your Contacts list. You can simply enter the contact's name into the search field and then tap the appropriate search result to access the information. The FaceTime app also has access to your Contacts list, so if you have set up FaceTime, and then conduct a Spotlight Search for a contact, you could be viewing the contact info from within the FaceTime app.

Edit an Existing Contact

Over time, the contact information for a co-worker, friend, or family member is subject to change. The Contacts app makes finding names, numbers and other important information easy so that you can edit existing contacts without a hassle. The virtual keyboard enables you to enter a contact on the spot, wherever you are.

If you use Contacts on your iPhone, editing contacts on your iPad follows a very similar procedure. If this is your first time using Contacts, like most things Apple, the app is very intuitive and quite simple to use. Understanding how to edit contacts enables you to quickly update information such as a contact's phone number or email address.

Edit an Existing Contact

1 Tap **Contacts** on the Home screen.

The Contacts app opens.

2 Tap the contact you want to edit.

iPad displays the contact.

3 Tap **Edit**.

● iPad displays the contact's data in the Info Screen. A red button (⊖) appears next to the data you can edit.

④ Tap the data field(s) that you want to edit and then make your edits.

The on-screen keyboard appears as you tap the field you want to edit.

Note: If you make a typo in the middle of a word, it can be hard to tap between the exact letters where it occurred. Hold your finger down on the word to access the magnifying glass and cursor. Move your finger to place the cursor in the exact location.

⑤ Tap **Done**.

Your iPad returns you to the All Contacts screen.

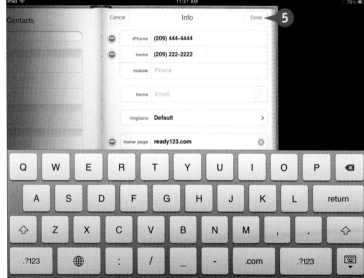

TIP

I have a lot of contacts. How do I quickly find the contact I need to edit?

You can use the Search field at the top of the All Contacts screen. As you begin to type the contact you are searching for, the results narrow until they match your search. To display all the contacts again, tap the ⊗ located in the search field to clear the search.

Assign an Email Address to a Contact

It may not be possible to acquire all the contact information from an individual in one meeting; so, naturally, you will have to add it later. Individuals commonly have a work and home number and also an email address for work and one or two for personal use. The Contacts app allows you to enter multiple email addresses. That way, you can make sure that you send your correspondence to the appropriate email address. The Contacts app makes it very easy for you to assign an email address to a contact.

Assign an Email Address to a Contact

1 Tap **Contacts** on the Home screen.

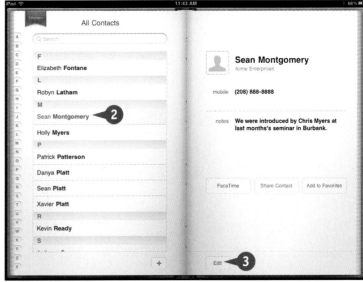

The Contacts app opens.

2 Tap the contact to whom you want to assign an email address.

The contact's Info screen appears.

3 Tap **Edit**.

The Info screen appears.

④ Tap the **Email** field and then type the email address.

A blinking cursor appears in the Email field when you tap it, and the on-screen keyboard appears.

● You can tap in the label field to change an email address's label.

⑤ Tap **Done**.

The email address is saved as part of the contact information.

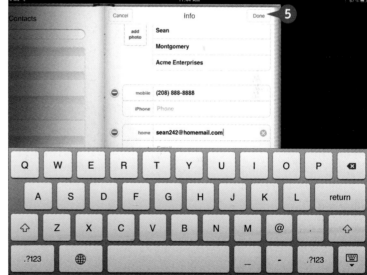

TIP

How do I save multiple email addresses?
As soon as you begin typing your first email address for a contact, a new Email field appears beneath it. The second field appears with a different label, so if your original email address has a Home label, iPad automatically labels the second email as Work and so on.

| home | sean242@homemail.com |
| work | seanm@myacme.com |

Assign a Web Address to a Contact

I t is now very common for individuals to be associated with multiple websites and not just a telephone number, email address, or street address. A typical person may have a company website and possibly more than one personal website. All of these web addresses may be of importance to you. Contacts has conveniently supplied you the means of entering multiple web addresses for a Contact. You can also change the label for an address to specify if it is a work or other type of web address. The Contacts app makes it very easy for you to visit an individual's website just by tapping the URL on the Info screen.

Assign a Web Address to a Contact

1 Tap **Contacts** on the Home screen.

The Contacts app opens.

2 Tap the contact to whom you want to assign a web address.

The contact's Info screen appears.

3 Tap **Edit**.

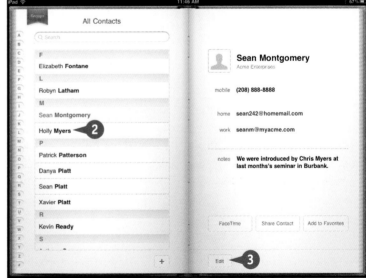

The Info screen appears.

④ Tap the URL field and then type the web address.

A blinking cursor appears in the URL field when you tap it, and the on-screen keyboard appears.

● You can tap in the label field to change the label for the web address. By default, the label field reads "home page."

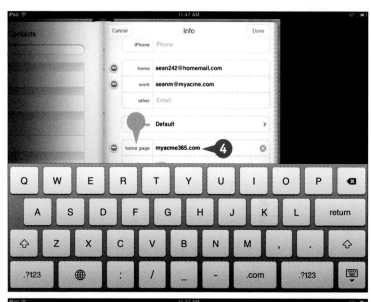

⑤ Tap **Done**.

The URL is saved as part of the contact information.

How do I assign multiple web addresses?

As soon as you begin typing your web address into the URL field, a new URL field appears beneath it. The second field appears with a different label.

home page	**myacme365.com**
home	**homewebsite.com**

What is the ringtone field located over the URL field all about?

Because iPad 2 is FaceTime capable, you can send and receive video calls. You can tap in the ringtone field to choose a default ringtone for a contact. When that particular contact calls you, you hear the specified ringtone.

Assign a Physical Address to a Contact

Assigning a street address to a contact enables you to save an individual's address and access it quickly whenever you need it. For your convenience, some of the apps also work together to help you simplify your efforts. When you assign a physical address to a contact, the Maps app gives you the added benefit of being able to locate that address on a map later. If you need to visit the contact, Maps can generate accurate directions to that contact's address stored on your iPad. You can easily add street addresses into the Contacts app so you can take advantage of these benefits.

Assign a Physical Address to a Contact

① Tap **Contacts** on the Home screen.

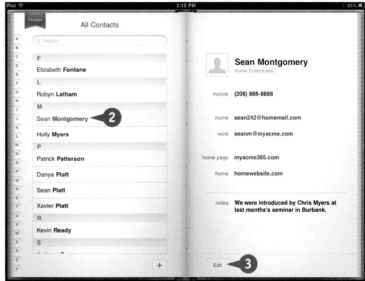

The Contacts app opens.

② Tap the contact to whom you want to assign a physical address.

The contact's Info screen appears.

③ Tap **Edit**.

The Info screen appears.

 Scroll down to tap the **add new address** field and then type an address.

A blinking cursor appears in the add new address field when you tap it, and the on-screen keyboard appears.

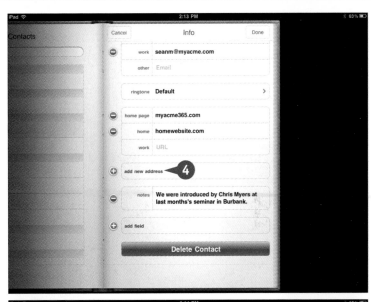

 Tap **Done**.

The address is saved as part of the contact information.

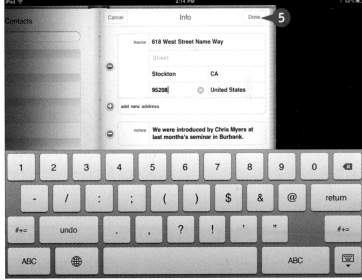

TIP

Can I see a map of the physical address I have assigned?
Yes. Another benefit to assigning an address to a contact is the fact that you can later use the Maps app to get a detailed map of the area just by tapping the address. To use the Maps app to quickly get directions to that location, you can tap the address for your contact.

home	**618 West Street Name Way**
	Stockton CA 95208
	United States

Create a Custom Label for a Contact

Whenever you assign information to your contacts, your iPad requires that you identify certain information, such as a telephone number or physical address, with labels, such as home, work, mobile, and so on. Occasionally, one of these labels may prove too generic for your purposes. Apple could not anticipate every possible label you may need for a contact, so they made it possible for you to customize your own. In this case, you can create a label for a field that contains temporary information for a project in just a few taps. Creating custom labels can help you better categorize your contact information.

Create a Custom Label for a Contact

1 Tap **Contacts** on the Home screen.

The Contacts app opens.

2 Tap the contact for whom you want to create a custom label.

The contact's Info screen appears.

3 Tap **Edit**.

The Info screen appears.

4 Tap the label for the contact data for which you will create the custom label.

Note: This task changes the label for an existing web address.

The Label menu appears.

5 Tap **Add Custom Label**.

The Custom Label menu and the on-screen keyboard appear.

6 Type a new label.

7 Tap **Save**.

The custom label appears next to the data on the Info screen.

8 Repeat steps **4** to **7** to create custom labels for other data fields if needed.

TIPS

Why can I not save my custom label for new data?
Before your iPad can save your custom label, you must edit or add the data and then save your work. Once you have typed your contact's data into the field, the custom label is saved along with the data in the All Contacts screen.

Do I have to re-create my custom label to use the same one again?
No. Once you create a custom label, you can access it again from the Label screen to use it for other contact data, such as phone numbers, email addresses, web addresses, and physical addresses.

Add Extra Fields for a Contact

When you add a new contact, by default, your iPad supplies you with only the basic data fields. Fortunately, your iPad has a collection of additional descriptive fields that you can access and apply to a contact's information. You can add extra fields, such as a prefix for Dr. or a suffix for Jr., Sr., and III. If one of your contacts goes by a nickname instead of a legal name, this is probably a detail of which you should be aware. The Contacts app also has a field option for Nickname. The choices for other fields include Job Title and Department. Extra fields come in handy when every detail matters.

Add Extra Fields for a Contact

1 Tap **Contacts** on the Home screen.

The Contacts app opens.

2 Tap the contact for which you want to add a new field.

The contact's Info screen appears.

3 Tap **Edit**.

The Info screen appears.

4 Scroll down and then tap **add field**.

The Add Field menu opens.

5 Tap a new field to add to the contact.

The Add Field menu closes, and the new field is added to the contact in the Info screen.

6 Type the information into the new field.

7 Tap **Done**.

Your iPad saves the new field for the contact and returns you to the All Contacts screen.

8 Repeat steps **2** to **7** to add fields for other existing contacts if needed.

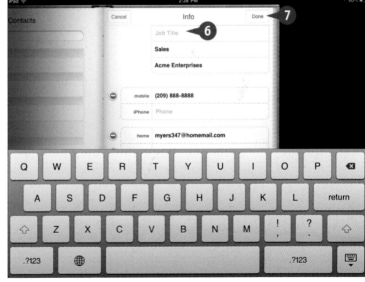

TIPS

Can I add a new field to a new contact?
Yes. But you need to type information into the empty fields before Contacts saves the new field. Follow these steps:

1 Tap the plus sign (+) on the contact's page.

2 Repeat steps **2** to **7** in this section.

What other types of fields can I add?
You can choose from 11 hidden fields: Prefix, Phonetic First Name, Phonetic Last Name, Middle, Suffix, Nickname, Job Title, Department, Instant Message, Birthday, and Date. The Birthday and Date fields can help you make sure that you do not miss birthdays or anniversaries.

Add Notes to a Contact

Sometimes, when you are adding an individual to your contacts list, it is very helpful to jot down some extra information about that person, such as where you met him or her, or the highlights of a recent meeting. Your iPad makes it easy for you to save important information such as this by enabling you to add notes to contacts.

An additional note can help you remember the specifics of a conversation that you had with an individual, if you have not talked in a while.

Add Notes to a Contact

1 Tap **Contacts** on the Home screen.

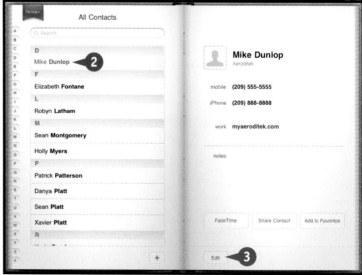

The Contacts app opens.

2 Tap the contact to which you want to add notes.

The contact's Info screen appears.

3 Tap **Edit**.

The Info screen appears.

④ Scroll down and then tap in the **notes** field.

The on-screen keyboard appears.

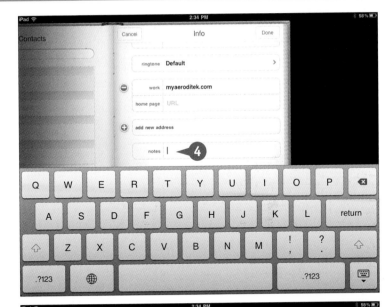

⑤ Type your notes.

Note: You can type faster by double-tapping the spacebar at the end of sentences and letting iPad add the period and the space at the end.

⑥ Tap **Done**.

Your iPad saves the notes for the contact and returns you to the All Contacts screen.

● You can tap the red button (⊖) that appears next to the note field in the Info screen to delete the notes if needed.

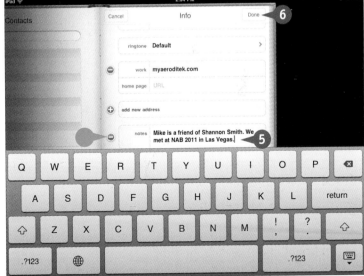

TIP

What are some other reasons for using notes?
Notes are great for quickly catching you up on extraneous information that may prove important to future interactions with that person. Perhaps you have met this person only once and were introduced by a fellow colleague. It may prove important in a future discussion to remember you share a mutual friend or acquaintance.

Add Photos to Contacts

Your iPad provides you with a surefire way not to forget the faces of important contacts by enabling you to add a personal photo to a contact. Because the iPad 2 has the ability to take photos, you can take a headshot on the spot. You can also sync a photo of a friend or colleague from your computer or use the camera connection kit to get photos onto your iPad. You can also download a photo from a web page or an email.

Follow these steps with the Contacts app open.

Add Photos to Contacts

1 Tap the contact for which you want to add a photo.

The contact's information appears.

2 Tap **Edit**.

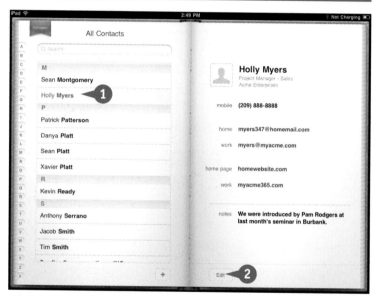

The Info screen appears.

3 Tap **add photo**.

4 Tap **Choose Photo**.

Your iPad displays your photo albums.

5 Tap the photo album that contains the picture you want to add.

The photo album opens.

6 Tap the photo that you want to use.

The photo enlarges in the Choose Photo dialog.

7 Move and scale the image so it looks the way you want in the contact.

Note: You can pinch and then open or close your fingers to increase or decrease the scale of the picture. You can also reposition the photo with your finger.

8 Tap **Use**.

The photo is inserted into the contact in the Info screen.

9 Tap **Done**.

Your iPad saves the photo with the contact and returns you to the All Contacts screen.

TIP

Can I assign a photo to a contact from the Photos app?
Yes. After you select the collection of photos from which you want to choose the photograph, you can tap the **Share** button ( ) located in the upper right corner of the screen to reveal the Assign to Contact option. Once you tap **Assign to Contact**, your list of contacts appears. Just tap a contact to assign the photograph.

Email Photo
Assign to Contact
Use as Wallpaper
Print
Copy Photo

Create Contact Groups

Creating contact groups is a great way to organize the many contacts you acquire. You can create a group to store a collection of similar contacts such as friends from work, family, career opportunities, or organization-specific groups. You cannot create groups directly on your iPad. You can create groups in other applications, such as Mac OS X Address Book, Yahoo! Address Book, Google Contacts, Windows Address Book, and Windows Contacts.

Once you sync contact groups to your iPad, you can easily add new contacts to a group from your iPad. Contact groups allow you to locate a list of similar contacts more quickly than wading through your entire list of contacts.

Create Contact Groups

1 Connect your iPad to your computer and launch iTunes.

2 Click your iPad in the Devices list.

3 Click **Info**.

4 Click the **Sync Address Book Contacts** check box (☐ changes to ☑).

Note: If you are syncing to a PC, click the **Sync Contacts with** drop-down menu to choose from the following options: **Windows Contacts**, **Google Contacts**, or **Yahoo! Address Book**.

5 Click the **Selected groups** radio button (◯ changes to ◉).

6 Click the groups you want to sync to your iPad (☐ changes to ☑).

● If you have a Yahoo! or Google account, you can click the sync check boxes (☐ changes to ☑) to add those contacts to the sync.

7 Click **Apply**.

8 Tap **Contacts** on the iPad Home screen.

9 Tap **Groups** on the All Contacts page.

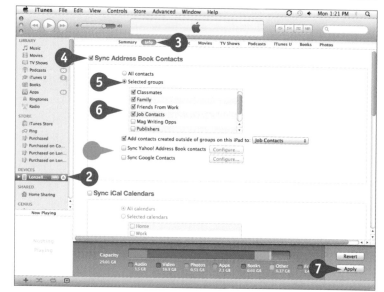

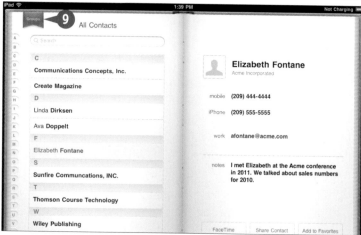

The list of groups synced to your iPad appears.

10 Tap the group for which you want to add a contact.

The contact group opens.

11 Tap the plus sign (+).

A new contact screen appears.

A blinking cursor appears in the box labeled First.

12 Tap each field and then type the information you have for the contact.

13 Tap **Done**.

Your iPad saves the information you have typed to the contact group.

TIP

Can I move contacts created outside of groups on my iPad into a group I just synced to my iPad?
You cannot accomplish this directly from your iPad, but you can during the sync process. Under the contact groups in iTunes, you can select the option to **Add contacts created outside of groups on this iPad to** a specified group listed in the drop-down menu. Besides manually copying the contact's information to a group on your iPad, this is the fastest way to group them.

Add Appointments to Your Calendar

Your iPad was designed for you to be mobile while still enabling you to manage the important stuff, such as doctor appointments, business meetings, and anniversaries. You can view your calendar by day, by week, by month, or even in list view. You can also see an overview of an entire month or a single day in detail. The Calendar app can display more than one calendar at a time so you can manage both your work and family schedules. Your iPad can help to ensure that you do not overlook important event dates.

Add Appointments to Your Calendar

Note: Follow these steps after you have already tapped **Calendar** on the Home screen and opened the Calendar app.

① Tap **Month**.

② Use the arrows to navigate to the month of the event.

③ Double-tap the date on the calendar on which the event is to occur.

The date opens in Day view.

④ Tap the plus sign (+) in the bottom right corner of the screen.

The Add Event dialog opens.

The Title field contains a blinking cursor.

5 Type the title for the appointment.

Note: You can also tap in the **Location** field to designate a location for the event.

The Start & End dialog opens.

6 Tap **Starts**.

7 Use the scroll wheels to set the date and time the appointment begins.

8 Tap **Ends**.

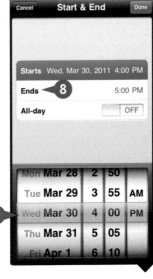

9 Use the scroll wheels to set the date and time the appointment ends.

10 Tap **Done**.

Your iPad saves the data and returns you to the Add Event dialog.

11 Tap **Done**.

The data is stored as an event, and your iPad returns to the Calendar screen. A dot appears under the date in the calendar to signify that the date has one or more events scheduled on it. iPad lists all the events for that day at the bottom of the Calendar screen.

TIP

How do I view the duration of the event for a particular date?
If you are unsure of how long you previously scheduled an event to last, you can follow these steps:

1 Tap the date in the calendar.

2 Tap **Day** to display a screen with the day, the date, the title of the appointment, and the duration of the event in blocks of time.

Edit an Existing Appointment

The details of your appointment, such as date and time, are always subject to change. Your iPad makes it easy for you to update your appointment schedules so your information is always up to date. The virtual keyboard enables you to edit an existing appointment on the spot, wherever you are. If you have a MobileMe account, you can make sure that your updated appointment information is synchronized with your other devices.

If you use the Calendar app on your iPhone, editing appointments on your iPad follows a very similar procedure. Knowing how to edit calendar appointments enables you to quickly update information so that you do not miss important appointments or events.

Edit an Existing Appointment

① Tap **Calendar** on the Home screen.

The Calendar app opens.

② Tap **Month**.

③ Use the arrows to navigate to the month of the event you want to edit.

④ Tap the date of the event you want to edit.

A banner appears on-screen for the event.

5 Tap **Edit**.

The Edit Event dialog opens.

6 Make your changes to the appointment.

Note: The end time for the event has been changed from 6 p.m. to 5 p.m. in this example.

7 Tap **Done**.

Your iPad saves the data and returns you to the Event screen.

TIPS

Is there a way for me to view all the appointments I have made?

Yes. You can tap **List** in the Calendar view to view all the appointments you have entered into the calendar. Appointments are listed in the order in which they occur. This is a quick way for you to view the details of an appointment.

Can I follow these instructions for editing an event in a view other than Month?

Yes. You can edit an existing appointment in Week view, Day view, and List view. Note that in List view, you would first tap the name of the event on the left of the screen and then tap the actual event on the right to access the Edit Event box. In List view, there is no banner with an edit option. The Edit Event dialog simply opens when you tap the event.

Set Up a Repeating Event

For those events that may occur routinely, Calendar enables you to enter the event one time and then schedule it to repeat at a regular interval. For example, if you want to schedule to meet a friend for lunch every day for a week while he or she is in town for business, you can create the event and schedule it to end in a week.

If an event occurs bi-weekly, Every Month, or Every Year, the Calendar app can accommodate your schedule. Knowing how to set up a repeating event keeps you from having to enter each event by hand.

Set Up a Repeating Event

1 Tap the date for the repeating event.

A banner appears for the event.

2 Tap **Edit** on the banner.

The Edit Event dialog opens.

3 Tap **Repeat**.

The Repeat Event dialog opens.

4 Tap the repeat interval you want.

5 Tap **Done**.

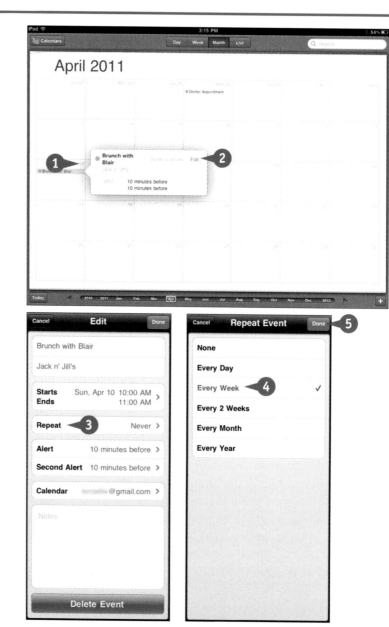

Calendar returns you to the Edit Event box.

6 Tap **End Repeat**.

The End Repeat dialog opens.

7 Use the scroll wheels to set the date you want the repeated event to end.

8 Tap **Done**.

Your iPad saves the data and returns you to the Edit Event screen.

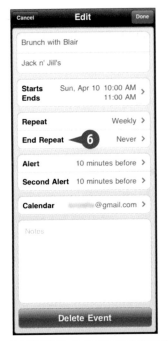

9 Tap **Done**.

The repeat data is saved.

Can I set an event to repeat indefinitely?
Yes. You can choose for the event to repeat indefinitely by tapping **Repeat Forever** in step **7**. If you should want this event to end, you have to manually edit the End setting for the repeated event.

Can I add comments to my events?
Yes. Calendar enables you to add notes to an existing event from the Edit screen. You can tap in the Notes field of the Edit Event or Add Event dialog to add details about the event or helpful reminders to help you manage your scheduled appointment.

Convert an Event to an All-Day Event

Typically, an appointment that you schedule with a doctor or for a meeting may last a few hours and not the whole day. Sometimes, the events that you schedule may not have clear start and end times, such as those for a conference, or a birthday, holiday, or anniversary. In these circumstances, you may need to block out an entire day for an important activity.

Calendar makes it easy for you to convert an event that you had previously scheduled for just an hour or two to an All-day event. When you specify an event as All-day, the event appears as such in each of the calendar views: Day, Week, Month, and List.

Convert an Event to an All-Day Event

1 Tap the date for the event.

A banner appears for the event.

2 Tap **Edit** on the banner.

The Edit Event dialog opens.

3 Tap **Starts**.

The Start & End dialog opens.

④ Tap the **All-day** option to the **On** position.

⑤ Tap **Done**.

Calendar returns you to the Edit Event dialog.

⑥ Tap **Done**.

The event is saved as an all-day event.

TIP

Are there any benefits to converting an event to All-day rather than marking it to last from 9 to 5?

One benefit is that it provides an easier way to view a calendar by Day. If you specify that an event lasts from 9 a.m. to 5 p.m. and then schedule other appointments between that time, Calendar displays the blocks of time on top of one another in the Day view, which makes the schedule hard to read. All-day events are shown separately.

Set an Alert for an Event

Now that you have entered events into your calendar, edited those events, set up repeated events, and marked some as All-day, you need to remember them. Adding an alert to an event is a great way to give yourself a little reminder before the event takes place.

By default, an alert is scheduled 10 minutes before the event. You can set an alert minutes, hours, or days before the event, and you can even set up more than one — just to be safe. Calendar issues a chime during the specified alert time and sends a message to your iPad screen. The alert message clears as soon as you unlock your iPad.

Set an Alert for an Event

1 Tap the date for the event.

A banner appears for the event.

2 Tap **Edit** on the banner.

The Edit Event dialog opens.

3 Tap **Alert**.

The Event Alert dialog opens.

④ Tap the amount of time before the event that you want to receive the alert.

⑤ Tap **Done**.

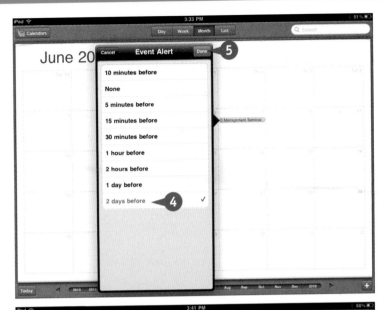

Your iPad returns you to the Edit Event dialog.

⑥ Tap **Done**.

Calendar saves the alert.

TIP

Why would I set up a second alert?

If you have a very busy schedule or are just forgetful, scheduling multiple alerts before an event can help you prepare yourself. A backup alert can act as a failsafe to ensure that you do not miss an event, even if you are preoccupied. If you scheduled an alert a day before the event, you can set up a second alert two hours before — just to be sure. You can set up a backup alert from the Edit dialog before tapping **Done** in step **6** by tapping **Second Alert**.

CHAPTER 9

Simplify Your Life with the iPad

Your iPad offers many tools that can help you simplify your life. Along with its many entertainment features, your iPad is also a personal digital assistant. iPad can also increase your productivity by helping you find the location of a hotel by using iPad's GPS capabilities or Wi-Fi triangulation, syncing with your MobileMe account, and running the Apple iWork suite of apps.

Explore Accessibility Options for the Visually and Hearing Impaired

The iPad possesses a range of accessibility features that makes it more accommodating for individuals who may be visually impaired, hard of hearing, or deaf or who may have a physical or learning disability. The iPad is equipped with a screen reader with adjustable speaking rate and 21 built-in voices that speak 21 languages. iPad supports playback of closed-captioned content and other helpful universal access features. Your iPad supports over 30 wireless Braille displays and features such as white on black text, and mono audio.

The accessibility options can be accessed by tapping **Settings** on the Home screen, and then tapping the **General** option.

Enlarge the Screen

The iPad makes it easy for you to magnify the entire screen within any app so you can read content more clearly. You have the ability to zoom up to five times the normal size while panning the page left or right or up or down to get a closer look at a specific area on-screen. The Zoom feature can be found by tapping **Settings** on the Home screen and then tapping the **General** option. The Zoom feature also works in apps that you download from the App Store. If you require a higher-contrast screen, your iPad enables you to change the display to white on black in any app.

Explore Closed Captioning

Many of the movies and podcasts that you download from iTunes support closed captioning for the deaf and hearing impaired. Your iPad can display subtitles and closed captioning for supporting movies and podcasts. You can search for closed-captioned movies on iTunes and then download them directly to your iPad, Mac, or PC.

Explore VoiceOver

The iPad uses a VoiceOver feature that enables you to simply hold your finger against the screen and hear a description of the item under your finger. To select an item, you double-tap it and then flick three fingers to scroll. The VoiceOver feature utilizes 21 languages and lets you control the speaking rate. VoiceOver

works with all the default apps installed on your iPad. A good thing to note here is that Apple has made it possible for software developers to create new apps that support the VoiceOver feature.

Explore Mono Audio

If you are hard of hearing in one ear, iPad enables you to play both the right and left audio channels through both headphones. This allows you to hear both channels in either ear at a given time. The Mono Audio feature offers the convenience of enabling you to enjoy full sound through one earpiece.

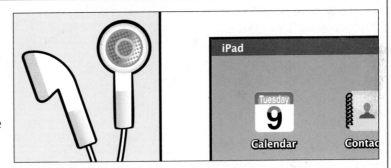

Explore Quick Access to Options

Regardless of which accessibility options you use the most, the iPad enables you to get to them by tapping **Settings** on the Home screen, choosing **General**, and then going into the Accessibility options. For the

visual and hearing impaired, you can configure your iPad to turn the VoiceOver, Zoom, or White on Black features off or on when you triple-click the Home button. This saves you a trip from going into Settings each time you want to turn on or off one of these features.

Display Your Current Location by Using Maps

The Maps app can help you pinpoint your exact location if you should ever find yourself in an unfamiliar location. You can simply tap **Maps** on the Home screen and then tap the **Tracking** button to have Maps show your precise current location. The location is represented by a blue dot on a detailed map. You can use the map to find another location, follow your route, or just to know where you are in relation to other destinations. By exploring what the Maps app can do for you, you can utilize it for your own unique purposes.

Display Your Current Location by Using Maps

1 Tap the **Tracking** button (◁) within the Maps app.

Maps asks if it is okay to use your current location.

2 Tap **OK**.

● Maps drops a blue pushpin on your current location.

Get Directions by Using Maps

The Maps app can help you get from point A to point B by providing you accurate directions. You can get step-by-step driving or walking directions to a specified destination by typing the addresses for the starting location and the desired destination. Maps can also provide up-to-date traffic information so that you can choose the best route.

You can conveniently get directions for locations listed in your Contacts list by tapping your friend's name into the destination field instead of an actual address. The Maps application has streamlined many helpful functions so that its use is intuitive.

Get Directions by Using Maps

1 Tap **Directions** in the Maps app.

The Start and End fields appear in the upper right, and the on-screen keyboard appears.

2 Type the starting address into the Start field.

3 Type the destination in the End field.

● Maps places a pushpin in the map for the start location.

● Notice that a Recents list appears, which displays a list of recent locations you have specified. As you begin to type, Maps makes suggestions for the address you are entering. The Recents list turns into Suggestions. If the location you want appears in the list, you can tap it to enter it into the field.

4 Tap **Search**.

● Maps provides directions at the bottom of the screen.

Note: You can choose to receive driving, public transit, or walking directions.

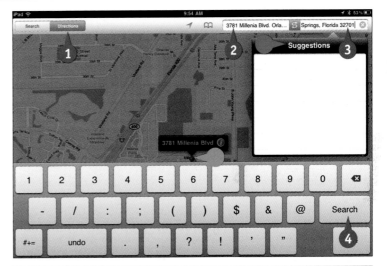

Specify a Location When You Do Not Have an Address

The Maps app can help you find locations for which you do not have an address. For example, you may know that a specific restaurant is located downtown, but you do not know how to get to downtown from your hotel. The Maps app enables you to add a pushpin where downtown is located on the map and then generate directions on how to get there.

Whether you are walking, driving, or using public transportation, Maps can help you get there by allowing you to specify the type of directions it generates. Maps also adds an estimated travel time.

Specify a Location When You Do Not Have an Address

1 Display the map of the city for which you want to specify a location.

Note: If you are currently in the city, you can tap the **Tracking** button (◀) to display the city you want.

Note: You can also tap **Search** and then type the name of the city you need.

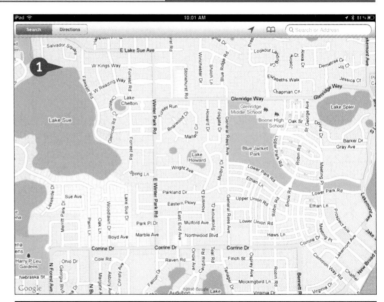

2 Pan and zoom the map with your finger to pinpoint the area you want to specify.

3 Tap the part of the screen that looks like a page curl in the bottom right corner of the screen.

The page curls, revealing the Map, Overlays, and Drop Pin settings.

④ Tap **Drop Pin**.

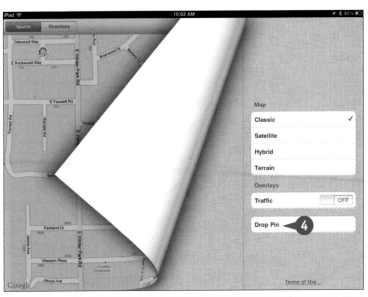

The Maps app drops a purple pushpin in the area you specified on the map.

⑤ Drag the purple pushpin to the location you want to specify on the map.

Note: You can now tap **Directions** and then type the address for your current location and add the specified location to the End field.

How do I find my way back from the specified destination to my original starting point?
You can find your way back to your original starting point by having your iPad reverse the directions for you. Tap the **Switch Start and End** button (🖺) located between the Start field and the End field under the Directions tab. The iPad generates directions so you can follow them back to your original destination. As with the previous directions, you can select directions for driving, public transit, and walking.

Display a Contact's Location

If the person's address that you need to reach is located in your contacts, you can avoid typing the address to generate directions on your iPad. Both the Contacts and the Maps apps enable you to display a map of a contact's location. Simply tap a contact's physical address in the Contacts list to display a detailed map with streets named and the destination marked with a pushpin. This feature is one of the many good reasons why you should keep your contact information up to date. All addresses from past directions generated in Maps appear in the Recents list for quick access, unless you have cleared the history.

Display a Contact's Location

1 Tap **Contacts** on the Home screen.

The Contacts app opens.

2 Tap the contact that you want.

The contact data appears.

3 Tap the address that you want to map.

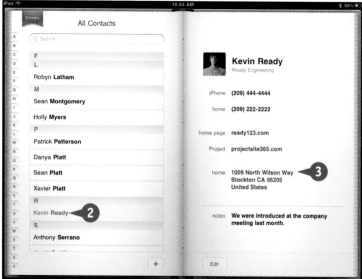

● The Maps app opens, displaying the contact's location.

④ Tap **Directions**.

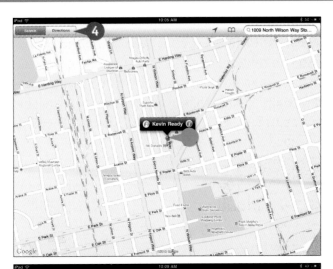

⑤ Type your current address in the Start field.

Note: If you tap in the field, you can choose an address from the Recents list that appears.

⑥ Type the contact's address in the **End** field.

⑦ Tap **Search**.

Maps provides you with directions to that location.

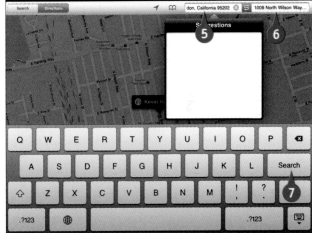

TIP

Can I display a map of the contact's location starting within the Maps app?
Yes. You can view a contact's location from within the Maps app by following these steps:

① Tap **Maps** on the Home screen.

② Tap **Search**.

③ Tap the **Bookmarks** icon (📖).

④ Tap **Contacts**.

⑤ Tap a contact in the list.

Bookmark a Location

Just like the iPad itself, the Maps app was designed to be intuitive, easy to use, and efficient. Typing the address for a destination that you do not visit often may not be a hassle, but having to do so continuously for locations that you frequently visit can get old. The Maps app can help with this. You can bookmark your most frequently used locations so you can quickly and easily retrieve directions. Over time, the majority of your frequently used directions can be available for fast access.

Bookmark a Location

1 Tap **Maps** on the Home screen.

The Maps app opens.

2 Tap **Search**.

3 Type an address in the Search field.

4 Tap **Search**.

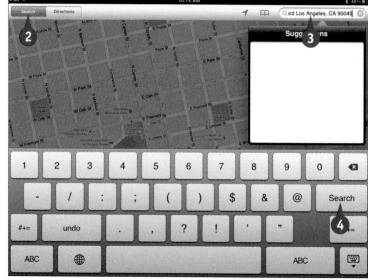

● The location is marked with a pushpin.

5 Tap the **Info** icon (ⓘ) to reveal details about the locations.

6 Tap **Add to Bookmarks**.

7 Modify the name of the bookmark if needed.

8 Tap **Save**.

Maps saves a bookmark of the location.

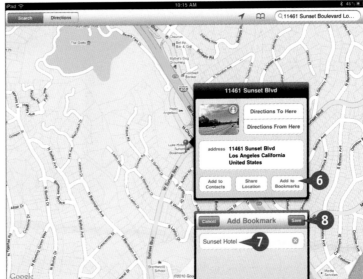

TIP

What if I forgot to bookmark a location but need to find directions quickly?
You can search in the Recents list. Tap the **Bookmarks** icon (📖) to open the Recents list, which contains previous directions you have generated in the Maps app. Check to see if the search you need appears in the list. If so, you can simply tap the address in the list, and your iPad can show you where the location is on the map as well as generate directions on how to get there.

Learn about MobileMe

MobileMe is an Apple service that enables you to sync your email, contacts, and calendar events to multiple devices, such as your iPad, iPhone, Mac, and PC. You can easily access important files while on the go, and if you should ever lose your iPad, MobileMe can help you find it. MobileMe allows you to sync web bookmarks across all your devices. If you bookmarked a site on your computer, you can access it on your iPad.

Your MobileMe account also enables you to publish photos that can be shared with friends and family in your MobileMe Gallery. A MobileMe account requires a basic membership fee of $99 a year, and you can read more about it and sign up at www.apple.com/mobileme. If you search other online resources, such as Amazon.com, you can find MobileMe memberships for less than $99 a year.

Sync Mail, Contacts, and Calendar Events

A MobileMe account offers a very simple way to organize your life online. MobileMe makes it easy for you to access data, such as your mail, contacts, and calendar event information, on multiple devices by storing it in what Apple refers to as a *cloud*, which amounts to networked servers. Whenever you log in to your MobileMe account, you are able to access and manipulate your data by using an online interface that you can easily access from your iPad, iPhone, iPod touch, Mac, or PC.

Publish to Your MobileMe Gallery

When you have a MobileMe account, you can upload photos from your iPad, iPhone, Mac, or PC so you can share them. A MobileMe Gallery enables friends and family to actively participate in the sharing of photos by downloading your photos or uploading their own. A MobileMe Gallery is a great way to showcase your favorite photos in a crisp, vibrant display.

Discover MobileMe iDisk

Along with your MobileMe account, you also have access to what is called iDisk, which is essentially a personal hard drive you can access on the web. You can access your iDisk by logging in at www.me.com, where you can upload, download, and organize files to your iDisk, just like you would any other hard disk drive. You can also open and edit files in another app such as any of the iWork apps: Keynote, Pages, and Numbers. The advantage of using your iDisk is that you can access it online from anywhere. Others can download your files when you use the Share feature in iDisk.

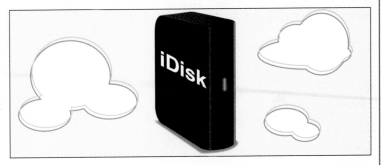

Find a Lost iPad, iPod, or iPhone

Your MobileMe account also comes with some helpful features you can use just in case you lose your iPad or iPhone. You can activate the Find My iPad feature in the MobileMe Settings on your iPad so that when you log in to www.me.com, you can log in to Find My iPad and display its location on a map. You also have the ability to remotely passcode-lock your iPad until it is found so no one can access your personal data.

Wipe Your iPad Remotely

Your iPad is home to a large amount of your personal information. Your personal information in the wrong hands can be catastrophic. MobileMe lets you remotely send a message to your iPad supplying your contact information, so if found, your iPad can be returned. If that does not work, along with passcode-protecting your device, you can initiate a remote wipe of your iPad. A remote wipe returns your iPad to its factory default settings, erasing all data. If you should find your iPad again, you can restore it with the data from your last backup.

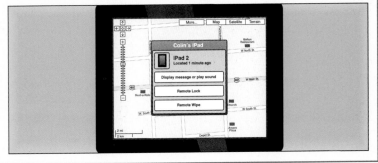

Set Up a MobileMe Account on Your iPad

A MobileMe account is a convenient service that is quick and easy to set up. A MobileMe membership supplies you web storage, photo hosting, contact/calendar syncing on multiple devices, web email, and a virtual drive that lets you share files anywhere. MobileMe also comes with a service that helps you find your iPad and iPhone, if you should happen to lose them. After you have signed up for a MobileMe account, you can easily configure your iPad to work with the account.

Set Up a MobileMe Account on Your iPad

1 Tap **Settings** on the Home screen.

The Settings screen appears.

2 Tap **Mail, Contacts, Calendars**.

The Mail, Contacts, Calendars screen appears.

3 Tap **Add Account**.

The Add Account screen appears.

4 Tap **MobileMe**.

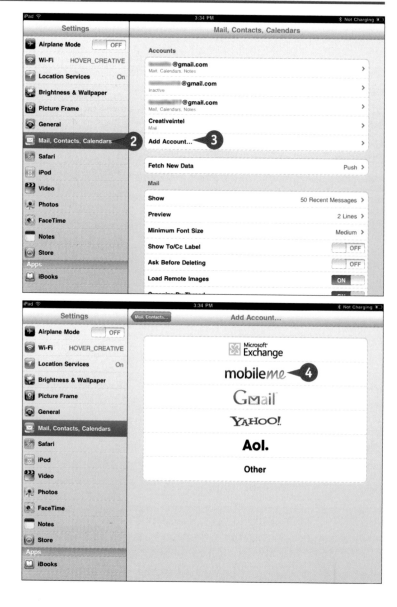

The MobileMe setup screen appears.

⑤ Type your MobileMe email address into the first field.

⑥ Type your MobileMe password into the Password field.

● If you do not have an Apple ID you can create one by tapping **Create Free Apple ID** and then following the prompts.

⑦ Tap **Next**.

MobileMe verifies the data you typed, and you are taken to the configuration screen.

⑧ Tap **OK** to allow MobileMe to use the location of your iPad.

⑨ Tap **Save**.

The Find my iPad feature has been activated and your MobileMe account has been added on your iPad.

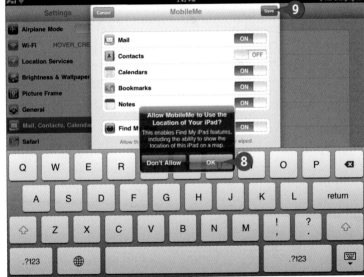

TIP

Once I sign up for an account and set up MobileMe on my iPad, is my account ready to sync to all my devices?

No. You still have to inform your cloud about all the other devices you will be using. You have to configure each device — your iPhone, Mac, or PC — with your MobileMe account before your information is synced to all devices. Once each device is properly configured, you can update information, such as a contact, with one device; the information is then sent to the cloud and updated for all the other devices.

Configure MobileMe Synchronization on Your iPad

If you keep important contacts and calendar information on multiple devices, you need each device to have the latest information. Your MobileMe account ensures that whenever new information is available for your email messages, contacts, and calendar events, it will be pushed to your iPad and other configured devices as soon as it is available. This keeps all your devices in sync. You can control the frequency in which new information is pushed to your iPad or decide to turn push off altogether on your iPad.

Configure MobileMe Synchronization on Your iPad

① Tap **Settings** on the Home screen.

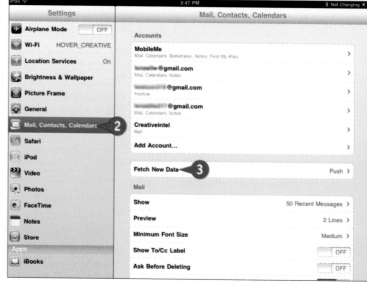

The Settings screen appears.

② Tap **Mail, Contacts, Calendars**.

The Mail, Contacts, Calendars screen appears.

③ Tap **Fetch New Data**.

The Fetch New Data screen appears.

④ Make sure that **Push** is in the **On** position if you want new information pushed to your iPad.

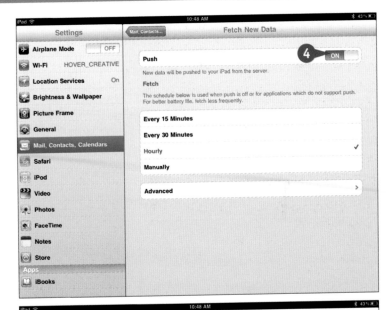

⑤ Tap the frequency with which your iPad will fetch new data.

● A check mark appears next to the chosen frequency.

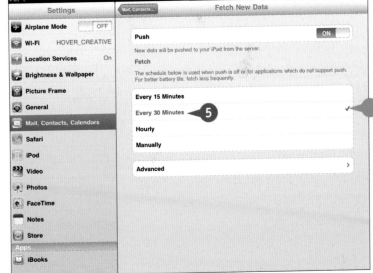

Configure MobileMe Synchronization on Your Mac

If you keep a considerable amount of information important to your daily operations on multiple devices, you need each device to have the latest information. An updated contact on your computer at home does not help you if the contact is outdated on your iPad and you need it while on the go.

After you have signed up for a MobileMe account, configuring your Mac for synchronization is a very straightforward process. You can choose to sync your bookmarks, calendars, contacts, and mail accounts with the system preferences so that your information is always up to date on your devices. Make sure that you have the latest version of iTunes.

Configure MobileMe Synchronization on Your Mac

① Click the Apple menu on the main menu bar.

② Click **System Preferences**.

The System Preferences window opens.

③ Click **MobileMe**.

The MobileMe preference pane opens.

④ Click the **Sync** tab.

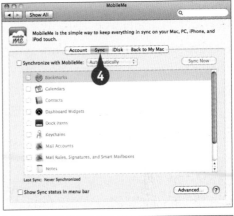

The sync options appear.

⑤ Click the **Synchronize with MobileMe** check box
(☐ changes to ☑) and then choose **Automatically**.

⑥ Click the **Bookmarks** check box (☐ changes to ☑).

⑦ Click the **Calendars** check box (☐ changes to ☑).

⑧ Click the **Contacts** check box (☐ changes to ☑).

⑨ Click the **Mail Accounts** check box (☐ changes
to ☑).

⑩ Click **Sync Now**.

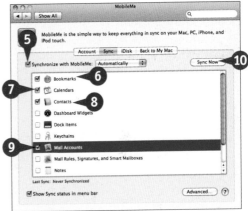

TIP

How do I access my iDisk on my Mac?
You can access your MobileMe iDisk (●) by opening any
Finder window. You can drag and drop files to save them
on your iDisk and manage folders — just as any other
hard disk drive. You also have the ability to locate
another MobileMe member's iDisk or Public folder by using
the Finder. You can password-protect your iDisk from the
MobileMe preferences and give only select users the
ability to read and write files to your personal iDisk.

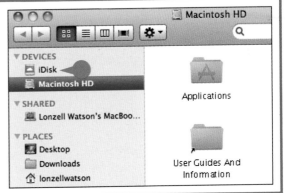

Configure MobileMe on Your PC

If you keep important data on multiple devices, you need each device to have the latest information. After you have signed up for a MobileMe account, configuring your PC for synchronization is a very straightforward process. You can choose to sync your bookmarks, calendars, contacts, and mail accounts with the system preferences so your information is always up to date on your devices. That way, when you update information on one device, all your devices receive the update.

Make sure you have the latest version of iTunes and that you have downloaded the latest version of MobileMe Control Panel for Windows.

Configure MobileMe on Your PC

① Click the **Start** menu.

② Click **Control Panel**.

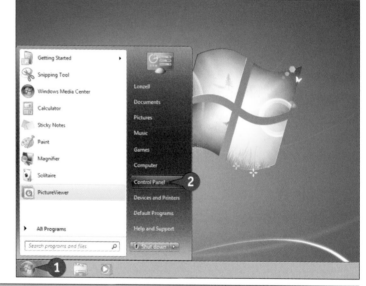

The Control Panel opens.

③ Click **Network and Internet**.

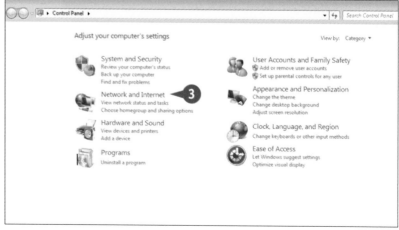

The Network and Internet
options appear.

4 Click **MobileMe**.

The MobileMe Sign In dialog
opens.

5 Type your member name and
password.

6 Click **Sign In**.

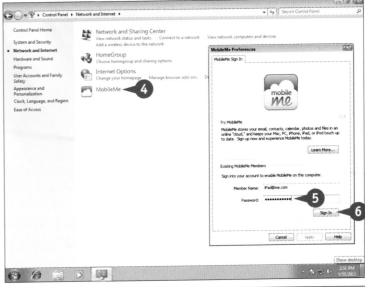

The MobileMe Preferences dialog
opens.

7 Click the **Sync** tab.

8 Click the **Sync with MobileMe**
check box (☐ changes to ☑)
and then choose **Automatically**.

9 Click the check boxes for
Contacts, **Calendars**, and
Bookmarks (☐ changes to ☑).

10 Click **Sync Now**.

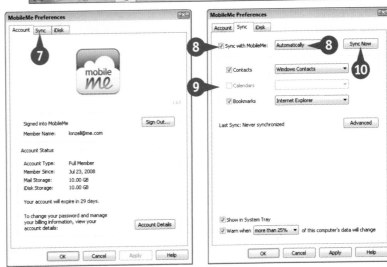

TIP

Can I review my MobileMe email messages with Outlook?
Yes. Keep in mind that you can always log in to your MobileMe account from your PC to check your email
from a web browser if you do not want to set up your email client. If you want to set up your email client,
you can go to the Tools menu in Outlook and then choose **E-mail Accounts** to access the Accounts Wizard
and set up MobileMe email in Outlook.

Send Photos to Your MobileMe Gallery

The high-resolution screen of the iPad 2, along with its portability and built-in back camera, makes it great for capturing, viewing, and sharing photos online, anywhere and anytime. Your iPad enables you to publish photos that you have synced to your iPad and captured with your iPad directly to your MobileMe Gallery. If something photo worthy happens around you, you can have it online in mere moments.

The MobileMe Gallery enables friends and family to actively participate in the sharing of photos by downloading your photos or uploading their own. If you do not have a MobileMe account, you can go to www.me.com to read more about it and to sign up.

Send Photos to Your MobileMe Gallery

1 In the Photos app, tap the group of photos that contains the photo you want to publish.

2 Tap the photo you want to publish.

The photo fills the screen.

3 Tap the **Share** button ().

4 Tap **Send to MobileMe**.

The Publish Photo screen opens.

5 Type a title for the picture.

6 Type a description.

7 Tap **Publish**.

The photo is published to MobileMe.

● A dialog opens, allowing you to view the photo you just published, tell a friend, or close the dialog.

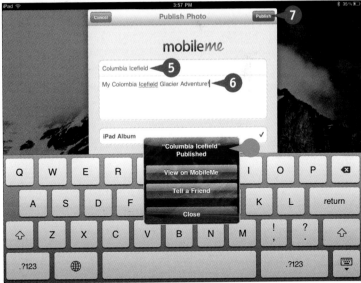

TIP

How do I view my MobileMe Gallery without having published something?

After you publish a picture from your iPad to your MobileMe Gallery, you are given the opportunity to visit the gallery with just a single tap of a button. You may want to visit your site without having posted something first. Because your MobileMe account exists in an online cloud, you can access it from any browser. All you need to know is your gallery's web address, which usually appears like this: http://gallery.me.com/ *yourusername*. To view a specific gallery, the web address looks more like this: http://gallery.me.com/ *yourusername*/#gallery. Make sure that you write down and possibly bookmark the address of your galleries.

Explore iWork

With Apple's iWork for the iPad you can perform real work on your iPad that not long ago could be achieved only on your computer. iWork is Apple's productivity app suite, which includes Keynote for presentations, Numbers for spreadsheets, and Pages for word processing and page layout. Each of these apps are currently available for your Mac, but these mobile apps have been redesigned and optimized for iPad.

Understanding the purpose of each piece of software in the suite can help you decide if iWork can make you more productive. These apps can be purchased separately for $9.99 each on the App Store.

Explore Keynote

Keynote makes it easy for you to create high-quality, professional presentations with a few taps of your finger. The Keynote app enables you to choose from professionally designed template themes to create your presentation. You can customize each presentation slide by swapping placeholder text and graphics with your own words and images. Choose from elements such as tables, charts, media, and shapes to add the finishing touches to your slides.

Explore Pages

Pages offers advanced tools for writing and easy page layout by using a collection of Apple-designed templates. You can use Pages to create high-quality résumés, brochures, school reports, or invitations. Pages enables you to add tables and charts to display important data in your documents as well as copy data from other iWork apps, namely Numbers.

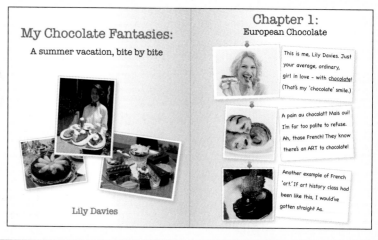

Explore Numbers

Numbers makes it easy for you to quickly create high-quality, attractive spreadsheets. Use the high-quality Apple-designed templates and easy-to-create formulas, tables, and charts to help you organize and plan. You can use Numbers to help you plan an event, save for retirement, track your diet, and even keep a journal.

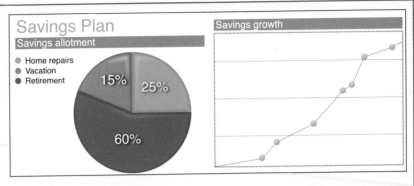

Work on iDisk

Keynote, Pages, and Numbers support MobileMe iDisk. What this means for you is that you can transfer your iWork documents directly to and from MobileMe iDisk from anywhere you have access to an Internet connection. For example, you can create your presentation in Keynote on your iPad and then save it to your iDisk. When you are ready to work again, you can access the file on your iDisk from your Mac to resume working.

Purchase iWork for the iPad

Each iWork app supports iDisk and has been redesigned for iPad so you can create professional presentations, word-processing documents, and spreadsheets with your fingertips. Each app is sold individually for $9.99 in the App Store, but you can also purchase the entire suite at once. If you already have the original iWork suite on your Mac, consider updating it to the latest version so that you can take advantage of iDisk support. The iWork apps for iPad are the most powerful productivity apps made for a mobile device, and they are easy to use.

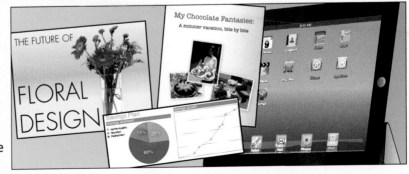

CHAPTER 10

Enhance Your iPad

Although the iPad comes with some amazing apps right out of the box, you can expand its capabilities by downloading new apps from the App Store. You can choose from thousands of innovative apps, ranging from games to productivity apps. There are also many accessories available for the iPad, including Smart Covers and the Apple wireless keyboard.

Explore the App Store

Software developers from around the world have developed thousands of apps to take advantage of the iPad, iPhone, and iPod technologies. If the iPad does not possess some of the functionality you would like, there may be an app for that. You can browse the App Store by category, such as Games, Entertainment, Utilities, Social Networking, Music, and Productivity. The list is too long to list them all here.

There are many free apps as well as more advanced apps that you have to pay for that you can download wirelessly to your iPad. To purchase apps in the App Store, you must have an iTunes Store account.

Access the App Store

You can access the App Store from your iPad by tapping the App Store icon or from your Mac or PC within the iTunes Store. Almost all the apps designed for the iPod touch and iPhone work with the iPad, so all you need to do is download them. You can also sync apps that you have previously downloaded for your iPhone or iPod touch to your iPad from your Mac or PC via the 30-pin dock connector.

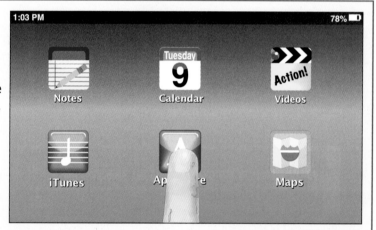

Find Apps in the App Store

Searching and downloading apps in the App Store is very similar to browsing for songs and albums in the iTunes Store. Once you tap the App Store icon, you can sort through content in a variety of ways, including Featured, Categories, Top 25, and Search. Choosing Featured lists the hot, new apps in the App Store, whereas Categories provides a more comprehensive search for apps. Use Categories to search content in collections such as Games, Social Networking, and Music. Top 25 lists the 25 most popular apps. You can also perform a keyword search.

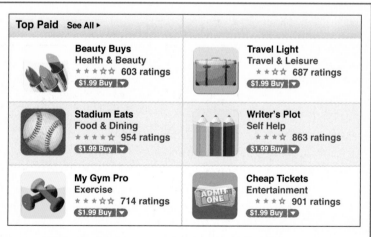

Download Video Games

Your iPad 2 has up to nine times the graphics performance of its predecessor. What this means is that you will notice smoother gameplay on your iPad 2. The App Store has many games for you to download and play on your iPad — some free and some that you have to pay for. Many of these games are specifically

designed to take advantage of the iPad motion sensor technology, allowing you to tilt the iPad to control aspects of the game on-screen.

Read and Post Reviews for Apps

Tens of thousands of apps are available for you to download to your iPad, so use your storage space carefully by reviewing apps before you download them. Reading descriptions and reviews is easy in the App Store. Tapping an app icon in the App Store immediately opens the app description, complete with screenshots from the app. The App Store uses a

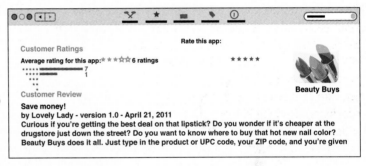

five-star rating system; tap in the rating fields to read customer reviews of the apps. You can post your own review for an app by tapping the **Write a Review** field located above the customer reviews.

Update Your Apps

As software developers continue improving their apps, they often release updates to the software you may have already downloaded from the App Store. The App Store notifies you when developers have released an update for the software you have previously downloaded by placing a red alert on the App Store icon located on the Home screen. The alert signifies how

many apps have updates by displaying a number. You can simply access the Apps Store and choose **Updates** to initiate the updates. You can choose to update individual apps or update each of them automatically.

Download Free Apps

You can take advantage of tons of free apps in the App Store. Many of them are shown in the Featured category alongside their paid counterparts. You can choose to filter your search and browse the Top Free iPad Apps section under the Top Charts category. Some apps have trial versions you cannot test drive before purchasing. Look for "Lite" versions of applications to test before you buy.

You need to set up an iTunes account before you can download apps in the App Store. Once you have created an account, you can download apps with just a few taps of your finger.

Download Free Apps

① Tap **App Store** on the Home screen.

The App Store opens.

② Locate the app you want to download and then tap **Free**.

The Free button changes to the Install button.

③ Tap **Install App**.

The App Store asks you to type your iTunes account password.

④ Type your iTunes username and password.

⑤ Tap **OK**.

The App Store begins to download the app. An icon for the app appears on the Home screen, along with a progress bar that tracks the download. The button changes from loading to installing.

Note: When the download is complete, loading changes to the name of the app.

The app launches.

TIPS

Can I play games that I downloaded from the App Store for the iPad on my computer?
No. The games and apps that you download from the App Store can be played only on your iPad, iPhone, and iPod touch. There may also be some apps made for the iPhone that are not compatible with the iPad. There are many iPad apps that will not play on the iPhone or iPod touch, such as Pages, Numbers, and GarageBand to name a few. Make sure that you carefully read the app description.

Can I create folders for apps on my iPad?
Yes. You can create folders on your desktop to group similar apps together. Simply press your finger on top of an app until all icons start to wiggle on screen. Drag the app over top of another similar app — for example, drag a news app on top of another news app. A folder is created automatically, and iPad even names it for you. You can change the name if you want and fit 12 apps into a folder.

Purchase and Download Apps

The iPad is not just about state-of-the-art hardware craftsmanship. Your iPad's true strengths can be found in the incredible software developed for it. The iPad comes with some truly amazing apps right out of the box, but some of the educational and productivity apps you will find in the App Store are simply amazing.

The App Store has a wide variety of sophisticated apps, some of which you have to pay for. The process for purchasing and downloading apps is almost identical to downloading free apps from the App Store. All purchases are made through your iTunes account.

Purchase and Download Apps

① Tap **App Store** on the Home screen.

The App Store opens.

② Locate the app you want to download and then tap the price.

The Price button changes to Buy App.

3 Tap **Buy App**.

The App Store asks you if you want to use an existing Apple ID or create a new Apple ID.

4 Tap **Use Existing Apple ID** if you already have an Apple ID.

The App Store asks you to type your iTunes account password.

5 Type your iTunes password.

6 Tap **OK**.

The App Store begins to download the app. An icon for the app appears on the Home screen, along with a progress bar that tracks the download. The button changes from loading to installing.

TIPS

Will I be charged twice if I attempt to download an app that I had previously paid for?
Usually not. When you attempt to download a previously purchased app, the App Store generally alerts you to this fact and asks if you would like to download it again for free. If you are rebilled for the second download, you can go to the app's information page located in the App Store and then tap **Report a Problem**.

Will I receive a receipt for my purchase?
Yes. The App Store emails you a copy of your receipt to the email address associated with your account. The process is not instantaneous, so it may take several days before you receive it. If you have made more than one purchase in a short period of time, you may receive a single receipt with several items listed. The App Store also sends you receipts for free downloads.

Move Apps from Your Computer to Your iPad

Your iPad is not the only portal in which you can access and download apps from the App Store. You can access the App Store in the iTunes Store under the App Store tab.

You cannot play downloaded apps from the App Store on your computer, but if you have purchased apps on your Mac or PC, you can sync those apps to your iPad as well as to your iPhone or iPod touch, if the apps are compatible and your devices are registered to your iTunes account. iTunes uses an interface that resembles your iPad Home screen so that you can manage your apps on your iPad.

Move Apps from Your Computer to Your iPad

① Connect your iPad to your computer.

② Launch iTunes.

iTunes opens.

③ In iTunes, click your iPad in the Devices list.

④ Click the **Apps** tab.

⑤ Click the **Sync Apps** check box (☐ changes to ☑).

6 Click the check boxes (☐ changes to ☑) next to the apps you want to sync.

● You can also drag apps from the list on the left to the iPad Home screen on the right and use those screens on the right to arrange your apps. In many cases, you may find this method preferable to getting into wiggle mode and then dragging apps from screen to screen.

Note: If you have downloaded apps for an iPhone or iPod touch that are not compatible with your iPad, iTunes deselects the check boxes (☑ changes to ☐) for those apps in the list.

7 Click **Apply**.

iTunes syncs the iPad with the apps you selected.

TIPS

Can I move apps off my iPad?

Yes. You can move apps off your iPad by deselecting the check box (☑ changes to ☐) next to the app in the list on the left. You can also navigate to the iPad Home screen on the right, position the mouse pointer over the app you want to remove, and then click the ⊗ that appears in the upper left corner. When you click **Apply**, the app is removed from the iPad.

Can I rearrange the apps on my iPad by using the iPad Home screen in iTunes?

Yes. You can drag app icons to rearrange them on the Home screen within iTunes. When you click **Apply**, the apps are rearranged on the iPad.

Check for Updates to Apps

I n order for you to keep the apps on your iPad up to date, you must update your apps when updates are available. The App Store notifies you when developers release a new version of an app that you have downloaded. You can perform updates from both your iPad and your computer.

If you already own an iPhone or iPod touch, then you are used to this process. If you are unfamiliar with this process, updating the apps on your iPad can be accomplished in just a few clicks. Updates are usually free.

Check for Updates to Apps

1 Tap **App Store** on the Home screen.

Note: A number appears over the App Store button to signify how many apps installed on your iPad have available updates.

The App Store opens.

2 Tap **Updates**.

The Updates screen appears with a list of all the apps that have available updates.

Note: You can access the Updates screen only if updates are available for your downloaded apps.

3 Check for updates.

Note: If all your apps are up to date, nothing appears in the list. If updates are available for apps on your iPad, you can tap an update in the list to read a description of the update you have chosen.

● You can update one app at a time, or you can choose to simply tap **Update All** to update all apps at once.

4 Tap to update an individual app.

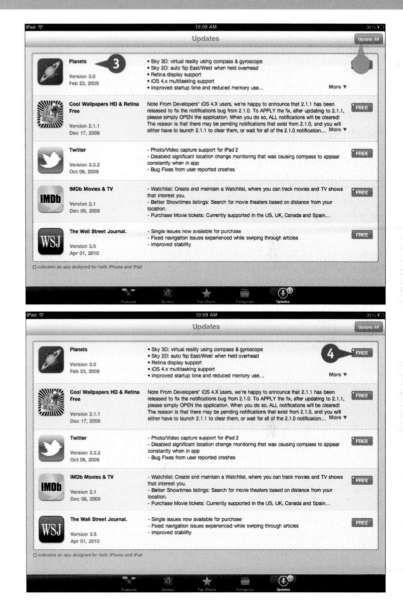

Can I update my apps from my computer?

Yes. You can update your downloaded apps from your Mac or PC by clicking **Apps** in the iTunes library. The icons for all the apps you have downloaded appear, with the number of updates available appearing in the bottom right corner. You can click **Updates Available** (●) to download available updates.

Accessorize Your iPad

Consider a Smart Cover

The Smart Cover enables you to protect that big beautiful screen that is the iPad 2 from dust and scratches, while still maintaining its sleek appearance. The Smart Cover attaches to your iPad 2 via magnets and covers only the screen. The Smart Cover can be folded so that you can position your iPad upright, tilt it into a typing position, or prop it up for movie time. Smart Covers come in ten different colors and are available in polyurethane and leather.

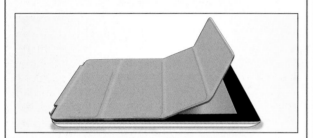

Protect Your iPad with an iPad Case

For a little more protection than the Smart Cover, the iPad has optional protective cases, like those for the iPhone and iPod, that help prevent its body and screen from becoming scratched or collecting dust. The iPad case not only protects the iPad, but it can also be used to situate the iPad in various positions so you can easily type, view photos, and watch movies for extended periods of time.

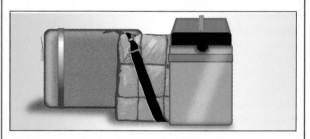

Charge Your iPad with the iPad Dock

Apple introduces a new dock stand for the second generation iPad that allows you to charge and sync your iPad. It also offers an audio line out port for connecting to powered speakers with an optional cable. You can also use other accessories with the dock, including the Apple Digital AV Adapter and the iPad Camera Connection Kit. A plain charging dock also comes in handy if you just need an extra charging dock at home or at the office.

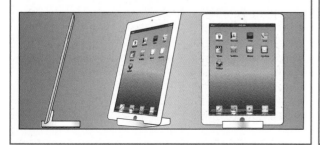

Explore the iPad Wireless Keyboard

Go wireless and invest in a keyboard that uses Bluetooth technology. The Apple Wireless Keyboard gives you the added convenience of actually typing with a physical keyboard while using the iPad. If you require a typing experience more similar to using a conventional computer keyboard, this may be the accessory for you. Users who perform extensive writing tasks may find the more tactile iPad keyboard a better alternative to the on-screen keyboard. The Apple Wireless Keyboard requires only two AA batteries.

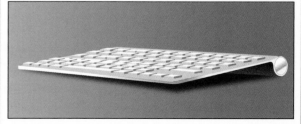

Learn about the 30-pin to HDMI Adapter

The new 30-pin HDMI adapter enables you to mirror your iPad out to a larger HDTV or a projector, so that your content can be viewed by a larger audience. This is great for presentations you create in Keynote on your iPad, or for teaching a class lesson from an app. One end of the adapter fits into the iPad and the other into the HDMI port of the HDTV. You can also use the second 30-pin to USB connector to charge your iPad as you conduct your business, so you do not run out of juice.

Discover the iPad Camera Connection Kit

The iPad Camera Connection Kit is composed of two connectors that can be attached to the iPad, allowing the iPad to directly download digital content from electronic devices. One connector allows you to download photos directly from a camera's USB cable, whereas the other allows you to download content from an SD card.

Use the iPad USB Power Adapter

The iPad power adapter is much like the adapter that comes with most Apple hardware. It gives you the flexibility of being able to charge your iPad through an electrical outlet. This may be a good option if you want to use the iPad for extended periods of time without being tethered to a shorter cable. The iPad 10W USB power adapter is 6 feet long.

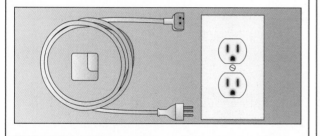

Consider an AirPrint-enabled Printer

Add an AirPrint-enabled printer to the mix and you can print your emails, web pages, photos, and documents wirelessly from your iPad. An AirPrint-enabled printer uses Wi-Fi to print your images, so you have no cables to connect, and also no software to download and no drivers. All you need is a working Wi-Fi network. Visit store.apple.com and hp.com for a list of AirPrint-enabled printers.

CHAPTER 11

Maintain and Troubleshoot the iPad

The occasional glitch can occur with any hardware device. In this chapter, you learn how to maintain your iPad and troubleshoot some common issues that may occur.

Check Automatic Sync

If you connect your iPad to your computer and iTunes does not respond, iTunes may not be set to automatically sync. You can click your iPad in the Devices list and then click the **Summary** tab to make sure that the **Automatically sync when this iPad is connected** check box is selected (☐ changes to ☑).

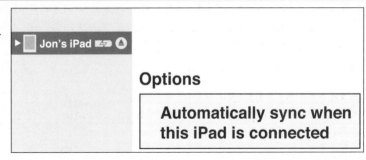

Check Free Space

If the space required for the content you want to sync exceeds the available space on your iPad, iTunes cannot perform the sync; a message usually alerts you about this. To avoid this issue, free up some space on your iPad to allow for the new content, or choose to sync less content to your iPad. Before you begin the sync process, you can check the space needed for the sync in iTunes as well as check your available space on your iPad under Settings.

Uninstall iTunes

As noted in the Apple Knowledge Base, on rare occasions, you may need to remove all traces of iTunes and related software components from your computer, and then reinstall iTunes. You can refer to the Apple support site for detailed instructions on how to uninstall iTunes and related components.

Index

Read Less–Learn More®

Visual®

There's a Visual book for every learning level...

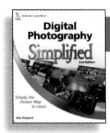

Simplified®

The place to start if you're new to computers. Full color.

- Computers
- Creating Web Pages
- Digital Photography
- Excel

- Internet
- Laptops
- Mac OS
- Office

- PCs
- Windows
- Word

Teach Yourself VISUALLY™

Get beginning to intermediate-level training in a variety of topics. Full color.

- Access
- Algebra
- Astronomy
- Bass Guitar
- Beadwork
- Bridge
- Car Care and Maintenance
- Chess
- Circular Knitting
- Collage & Altered Art
- Computers
- Crafting with Kids
- Crocheting
- Digital Photography
- Digital Video
- Dog Training
- Drawing

- Dreamweaver
- Excel
- Flash
- Golf
- Guitar
- Hand Dyeing
- Handspinning
- HTML
- iLife
- iPad
- iPhone
- iPhoto
- Jewelry Making & Beading
- Knitting
- Lightroom
- Macs
- Mac OS

- Office
- Outlook
- Photoshop
- Photoshop Elements
- Piano
- Poker
- PowerPoint
- Quilting
- Scrapbooking
- Sewing
- Web Design
- Windows
- Wireless Networking
- Word
- WordPress

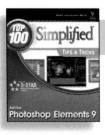

Top 100 Simplified® Tips & Tricks

Tips and techniques to take your skills beyond the basics. Full color.

- Digital Photography
- eBay
- Excel

- Google
- Office
- Photoshop

- Photoshop Elements
- PowerPoint
- Windows

...all designed for visual learners—just like you!

Master VISUALLY®

Your complete visual reference. Two-color interior.

- 3ds Max
- Creating Web Pages
- Dreamweaver and Flash
- Excel
- iPod and iTunes
- Mac OS
- Office
- Optimizing PC Performance
- Windows
- Windows Server

Visual Blueprint™

Where to go for professional-level programming instruction. Two-color interior.

- ActionScript
- Ajax
- ASP.NET 2.0
- Excel Data Analysis
- Excel Pivot Tables
- Excel Programming
- HTML
- JavaScript
- Mambo
- Mobile App Development
- Perl and Apache
- PHP & MySQL
- SEO
- Ubuntu Linux
- Vista Sidebar
- Visual Basic
- XML

Visual™ Quick Tips

Shortcuts, tricks, and techniques for getting more done in less time. Full color.

- Beading
- Crochet
- Digital Photography
- Excel
- Golf
- Internet
- iPhone
- iPod & iTunes
- Knitting
- Mac OS
- Office
- Paper Crafts
- PowerPoint
- Quilting
- Sewing
- Windows
- Wire Jewelry

Visual™
An Imprint of ⊕WILEY
Now you know.

For a complete listing of Visual books, go to wiley.com/go/visual